THE
PERSONAL
LIBRARIAN

ALA purchases fund advocacy,
awareness, and accreditation programs
for library professionals worldwide.

THE PERSONAL LIBRARIAN
Enhancing the Student Experience

RICHARD J. MONIZ JR. and **JEAN MOATS**

EDITORS

**Joe Eshleman, Valerie Freeman,
Jo Henry, and David Jewell**

CONTRIBUTORS

An imprint of the American Library Association

CHICAGO 2014

© 2014 by Richard J. Moniz Jr., Jean Moats, Joe Eshleman, Valerie Freeman, Jo Henry, and David Jewell.

Any claim of copyright is subject to applicable limitations and exceptions, such as rights of fair use and library copying pursuant to Sections 107 and 108 of the U.S. Copyright Act. No copyright is claimed for content in the public domain, such as works of the U.S. government.

Printed in the United States of America

18 17 16 15 14   5 4 3 2 1

Extensive effort has gone into ensuring the reliability of the information in this book; however, the publisher makes no warranty, express or implied, with respect to the material contained herein.

ISBNs: 978-0-8389-1239-3 (paper); 978-0-8389-1240-9 (PDF); 978-0-8389-1241-6 (ePub); 978-0-8389-1242-3 (Kindle). For more information on digital formats, visit the ALA Store at alastore.ala.org and select eEditions.

Library of Congress Cataloging-in-Publication Data
The personal librarian : enhancing the student experience / Richard J. Moniz Jr. and
    Jean Moats, editors ; Joe Eshleman, Valerie Freeman, Jo Henry, and David Jewell,
    contributors.
        pages   cm
    Includes bibliographical references and index.
    ISBN 978-0-8389-1239-3 (print : alk. paper) — ISBN 978-0-8389-1241-6 (epub) —
ISBN 978-0-8389-1240-9 (pdf) — ISBN 978-0-8389-1242-3 (kindle)
        1. Academic libraries—Relations with faculty and curriculum. 2. Academic librarians—
    Professional relationships. 3. Information literacy—Study and teaching (Higher) 4. Library
    orientation for college students. 5. Academic libraries—Marketing. 6. Academic libraries—
    United States—Case studies. I. Moniz, Richard J., editor. II. Moats, Jean, editor.
        Z675.U5P472 2015
        025.5'677—dc23   2014014990

Cover design by Krista Joy Johnson. Cover images © Shutterstock, Inc.
Text design in the Chapparal, Gotham, and Bell Gothic typefaces.

♾ This paper meets the requirements of ANSI/NISO Z39.48-1992 (Permanence of Paper).

Contents

Acknowledgments

THE AUTHORS WOULD LIKE TO OFFER OUR THANKS AND PRO-found gratitude to all of our colleagues at Johnson & Wales University and at various other institutions (Nancy Bellafante, Jenna Freedman, Kelly Lawton, Shannon O'Neill, and Laura Heinz especially come to mind in this regard). We regularly interacted with librarians and other educators who were willing to share their time and expertise. We would like to offer an extra special thanks to Peter Lehmuller, Justin Herman, Mason Bissett, Jan-Marie Lanuzza, Lisa Kendall, Susan Flaherty, Brian Mooney, John Maas, Emily Seel-binder, Mark Norman, Kenny Harmon, Daphne Thompson, Joan Geller, Patricia Childress, Alana Sherrill, Michael Stephens, Pat MacEnulty, Fernanda Tate-Owens, Vicki Cleveland, Amanda Winar, Ann-Marie Townley, Martha Griffin, Catherine Posey, Cheryl Murray, Kamisha Kirby, Bob Caldwell, and Stephanie Teasley. Collectively, they inspired, assisted, partnered, and encouraged us in developing our personal librarian program and this book. We would also like to thank Johnson & Wales University's Dean of Libraries, Dr. Rosie Hopper, and the Charlotte Campus's Vice President and Academic Dean, Dr. Tarun Malik, for their continued encouragement and leadership. Also, without the support and ongoing assistance of Jamie Santoro, our editor at ALA, this book would not exist (also critical was the assistance of Amy Knauer and her team when we reached the final stages). Authors Jo, Joe, and Richard would also like to thank Rachel Chance for all of her guidance and assistance with our previous ALA publication, *Fundamentals for the Academic Liaison* (as well as Rob Christopher's efforts to get the word out about it). Last but not least we would like to thank all of the students who come to us with open minds, a willingness to learn, and a desire to be successful in their chosen careers. We wish them all the best and hope that the personal librarians here at Johnson & Wales University and those established elsewhere contribute in some small way to this process.

1
The Origin of the Personal Librarian Concept

I WALKED INTO A LOCAL RESTAURANT SOME TIME AGO AND WAS greeted by a young woman who looked very familiar. As she took my order she blurted out, "I know who you are! I know who you are! You're my personal librarian!" I came back to the library that day, relayed the story, and began chatting with the other librarians who had also been involved in this new program. It turns out that, while we hadn't met with large numbers of students, we had all conversed with some who had recognized us from our role as their personal librarian. Many were as excited as this student whom I had seen at the restaurant. Some of us had met one-on-one with students who sought us out sometimes after class (we had at least one in-class session with students assigned to us), creating a rare opportunity to spend more focused time getting to know specific students while assisting them with their various research projects. We collected feedback in numerous classes and in a variety of ways through surveys, blogs, and quizzes. The following comment from one student stood out as being especially comprehensive and representative of other students' opinions in the sentiment it expressed:

> I have taken a few things away from having the resources of the library shown to me today. For one I now have a certain place where I can find information that isn't on Google. I feel I wasn't great at doing citations, but I am happy to see that I have a tab where I can relearn how to do citations in MLA format again. I feel a lot more confident with my research paper now since I have a few databases to choose from. . . . I also like the fact if I have a question about anything on the website or my research, I can have a direct link to e-mail *my librarian* [emphasis added] to help me out. . . . Having these resources shown to me and how to use them makes me feel less stressed about writing this research paper.

The response from faculty was likewise overwhelming. It seemed as though every time one of us attended a meeting outside the library or walked into the academic building where our classrooms are located we had faculty and staff patting us on the back saying, "Way to go with the personal librarian program! What a great idea!" The funny thing is that it took us a little while to digest the feedback, and it came as a bit of a shock because we had not made wholesale changes to what we were already doing. Rather, we took what we had been doing, changed our thinking a little, added to our existing approach in very targeted and specific ways, and then marketed it slightly differently than in the past. What we are here to tell you is that you can do this too. You can adapt our personal librarian program for your institution, as is discussed in various ways in this chapter. This does not mean throwing out the good things you have already been doing. It just means adapting a slightly different philosophy of service and incorporating some tweaks and changes that make sense for you and your institution. This will add to your success, the success of your library, and, most important, the success of your students. You can do this!

WHERE DID THE PERSONAL LIBRARIAN CONCEPT COME FROM?

While the concept and implementation of personal librarian programs are relatively new, the program and idea itself represent an exciting historical evolution in relation to library services in higher education. This chapter seeks to expand upon some of those developments and place a personal librarian program within its appropriate contemporary context. What should stand out to the reader is that what academic librarians have been doing all along has proceeded in a very logical progression toward the implementation of this type of idea. Foremost in our lead-up to the personal librarian concept, the development and shift of emphasis on information literacy that became especially strong after the turn of the century cannot be understated. Indeed, the shift to information literacy is in some ways the beginning of a tendency to focus more on developing the skills of our *individual* patrons as opposed to guarding a warehouse of books and knowledge. Another relatively recent development in the history of the library profession has been the implementation and continuous development of electronic resources. Twenty years ago most libraries focused their efforts on physical resources. Much has changed in that regard, as now most libraries offer access to online databases, streaming videos, e-book collections, and other virtual resources that dwarf physical collections. The rapid development of online resources coupled with the development of hybrid classes, online classes, learning management systems (such as Moodle and Blackboard), and Massive Open Online Courses (MOOCs) has led to a radical shift in the perception of library services and how they are experienced by users, administrators, and other key stakeholders. MOOCs in particular are addressed in some detail in the final chapter because these online courses, typically open to anyone and taught by some of the best professors in the world, are changing the higher education landscape altogether. Likewise, the role of academic library liaisons, while always critical to the success of academic library services, has shifted more from knowing the resources in a given area (although this is still important) toward establishing and building strong personal relationships with faculty in a given department, understanding faculty needs, and being able to assist faculty in new and often creative and collaborative ways. Finally, the personal librarian concept finds itself being born roughly within the context of an ever-increasing appreciation for retention in higher education. Businesses have always known the great value of keeping a customer relative to expending significantly more resources trying to find a new one. Higher education has shifted from placing bodies in seats toward making sure *individual* students receive a higher quality education and are better skilled and prepared for success both as they progress through college and as they make their way in the world beyond. As stated, the concept of the personal librarian has arisen in a specific context, one that is explored briefly in the next section and then in further detail throughout this book.

INFORMATION LITERACY

While the phrase *information literacy* and the concept in its root form date back to 1974, they took some time to gain widespread acceptance within the profession. According to Kathleen Spitzer, the development of computers in the 1980s and the realization that more information was and would become increasingly available necessitated the development of a new emphasis on *individual* user skills. Indeed, a report issued by the American Library

Association in 1989 recognized the need for information literate citizens who could maneuver their way through information and data that were rapidly becoming available.[1] According to the Presidential Committee on Information Literacy's Final Report:

> How our country deals with the realities of the Information Age will have enormous impact on our democratic way of life and on our nation's ability to compete internationally. Within America's information society, there also exists the potential of addressing many long-standing social and economic inequities. To reap such benefits, people—as individuals and as a nation—must be information literate. To be information literate, a person must be able to recognize when information is needed and have the ability to locate, evaluate, and use effectively the needed information. Producing such a citizenry will require that schools and colleges appreciate and integrate the concept of information literacy into their learning programs and that they play a leadership role in equipping individuals and institutions to take advantage of the opportunities inherent within the information society. Ultimately, information literate people are those who have learned how to learn. They know how to learn because they know how knowledge is organized, how to find information, and how to use information in such a way that others can learn from them. They are people prepared for lifelong learning, because they can always find the information needed for any task or decision at hand.[2]

In higher education most of us come into contact with information literacy through the Association of College and Research Libraries' (ACRL) "Information Literacy Competency Standards for Higher Education." While specific outcomes and performance indicators may be found at the ACRL website (www.ala.org/acrl/standards/informationliteracycompetency), they all break down into five basic Standards, which are discussed in much greater detail in this book, especially in how they relate to a personal librarian concept or program. In a nutshell, however, they amount to understanding that one has an information need, searching for information, evaluating it, and then using it in an ethical manner.[3]

Beyond its philosophical underpinnings, as so eloquently expressed in the Presidential Report quoted earlier, an emphasis on information literacy itself in a very practical way did not develop from thin air. Librarians had been assisting users all along and teaching bibliographic instruction sessions as well dating as far back as the 1800s.[4] What changed in the late twentieth century was a much greater realization that new and higher order thinking skills would be necessary to navigate the increasingly complex information environment. These skills, as noted, needed to be more comprehensive than simply showing students where the books are or telling them which resources to use. Rather, the idea was to create lifelong learners and critical thinkers capable of navigating information needs and concepts on their own after completing their degree program. According to Daniel Brendle-Moczuk, the goal is fairly lofty and includes instilling curiosity, desire, and the ability to become self-motivated alongside the traditional skills we have taught in the past.[5] It should be noted that while a revision of ACRL's Standards is under way, the same basic philosophy captured here by Brendle-Moczuk will remain central.

These Standards and information literacy in general in connection to personal librarian programs are expanded upon in a later chapter. It should be noted, however, that while information literacy has been around for some time, its implementation still varies widely from one college or university to the next. One debate from the onset of the information literacy movement that seems to be still ongoing is whether it is in some sense a "separate" set of skills that can be taught in a specific term-length information literacy course. While these types of classes are by no means uncommon, the more prevalent approach appears to be integrating ACRL's Standards as stated earlier into the curriculum itself such that they become interwoven in some fashion. For example, librarians might provide instruction in a wide variety of classes in an attempt to connect information literacy outcomes to related outcomes for a specific course. This integration can actually occur in a number of ways, which are touched upon in a later chapter. This widespread integration in turn creates numerous other challenges, such as how to assess information literacy skills, how to assess information literacy–related instruction, and how to scaffold information literacy skills across a student's college career or experience. The list seems endless, and the debates remain vibrant. In contrast to the perception that librarians are somehow obsolete, any thoughtful examination of information literacy and its complexities and possibilities makes it very clear how critical the instruction role is in relation to library services. Contextually, it is also important for us to understand, in relation to the development of a personal librarian program, that the information literacy debate includes the idea that our intent should be to assist *individual students* and to do so beyond a quick reference desk interaction. Personal librarian programs, as are defined and described in this book, likewise focus on the library user as opposed to the resources and build a bridge such that a student's skills are established and developed over time.

ONLINE COURSES AND EMBEDDED LIBRARIANSHIP

While correspondence courses have been around since the 1800s, the development of the Internet and web technology has led to a massive amount of online course offerings. These offerings grew organically from the experimentation that had occurred with the use of television and radio as well as fax machines and videocassettes. Yet, the Internet obviously offers many greater possibilities than these mediums of the past. According to Margaret Morabito, it was fairly typical for colleges and universities to begin experimenting with at least adding some online components to classes in the 1990s.[6] By 2011, a Pew research report indicated that 77 percent of institutions of higher education were offering some online course options. However, it is worth noting that while this option was available in some fashion to most students in 2011, it was still only a small fraction of what constituted a typical student's work. The institutions reported that only 15 percent of their students had ever taken an online course.[7] This number is expected to change dramatically over time. In fact, what we are seeing in the current higher education marketplace seems to bear this out. According to one report, the Learning Management System (LMS) market, targeting online courses and e-learning, is expected to grow from $2.55 billion in 2013 to $7.83 billion by 2018.[8] Additionally, many colleges and universities now regularly offer hybrid courses (which utilize an LMS at some level), at minimum, as well. These courses utilize online learning platforms such as Blackboard or Moodle but also combine the online with in-person components.

At minimum, *embedded* means to be integrated into an online class and thus connected to each student. Adding a librarian virtually into a course is typically something that instructors can do themselves or with the help of the institution's information technology department or an instructional technology staff person. The librarian is typically given access to course content such as the syllabus, discussion boards, announcements, and other relevant documents. By going one step further than one-shot instruction, David Shumaker, a noted scholar of embedded librarianship, states that embedded librarians "deliberately build relationships—with faculty, with students, with the marketing department, with a research team, or with any other user group."[9] Proximity can also be a component. That is, librarians can be located physically near the faculty whose class they are embedded in (perhaps even in an office in their department). According to Kathy Drewes and Nadine Hoffman, "A librarian's physical and metaphorical location is often what defines them as embedded."[10] That said, most authors recognize that *embedded* usually refers to being connected to the class in a virtual sense. Being connected in this manner allows the librarian to view assignments and posts and to interact with the students at a closer one-on-one level and with a deeper understanding of course content and needs. The development of online classes coupled with the ability to embed in a class has directly led to a greater ability to personalize library services for individual students, as is explained in this text. This is especially so for both purely online as well as hybrid courses.

HISTORICAL ROLE OF ACADEMIC LIBRARY LIAISONS

Librarians have always seen their role as assisting people directly with research in addition to their other basic information needs. It became evident in the early days of higher education in America that by paying special attention to the needs of faculty, librarians were indirectly providing a great deal of assistance to students as well. As such, many libraries have created and currently maintain formal library liaison programs or less formal assignments of a similar nature. It is common for a given department or area to have a librarian assigned who is concerned about that specific department's course-related needs. This librarian might also assist faculty members with personal research projects. There is a great deal more about academic library liaisons later in this book, as their development has led to our ability to implement a personal librarian program and there is much experience that may be transferred.

A key point needs to be made here. The intent in a good liaison program is to establish long-term, one-on-one connections and relationships between area faculty and librarians. In this sense, the connection and overlap with the personal librarian idea should be obvious. Good relationships between the faculty and librarians almost inevitably lead to a better experience for students. It is, however, the students themselves who are targeted in a personal librarian program for the establishment of ongoing, long-term relationships.

RETENTION EFFORTS

While no chapter in this book is dedicated entirely to the broader topic of student retention, it has had a demonstrable impact on the development of personal librarian programs; thus, a discussion of it is weaved throughout this text. For those new to the concept, student retention is, strictly speaking, a measure of how many students an institution retains from freshman to sophomore year (although many people also use it as a generic term encompassing a student's attendance all the way through to degree completion). The second chapter explores in more detail how retention efforts led directly to the establishment of a personal librarian program at Johnson & Wales University's Charlotte campus, for example. In the meantime, it is worth pointing out that in a recent study Gaby Haddow discovered that, at least to some extent, logging into library resources more frequently correlates with students being retained.[11] While the dynamics are unclear in some ways and the library may seek to target students through a variety of approaches, it does make sense that students who have a positive relationship with the library staff and library resources will experience less frustration and have a greater chance of persisting and being successful in college. Certainly, library resources and librarians in general contribute in a variety of ways to student retention. In relation to personal librarian programs specifically, other studies have shown that it is the personal connections among students, faculty, and staff that are most effective in ensuring that students are successful in college.

Certainly, the positive impact of partnering faculty and students in research is well-known. A 1998 study by Biren Nagda and colleagues indicates that students, especially at-risk students, were better retained when partnered with faculty for research projects. After referring to the work of Tinto, a well-known scholar within the discipline of research in higher education, Nagda states, "A firmer implementation of the integration principle would, therefore, involve students in a focused activity that is at the heart of the institution's mission, one that counteracts the individual's feelings of being socially and intellectually isolated from the institution."[12] This is exactly the intent of a quality personal librarian program, integrating the students' library experience and building their skills and confidence while providing a personal connection to resources and another person. While "regular" faculty connect and communicate with students on a regular basis, this is not always the case for librarians. So, how can we make sure that students connect personally with librarians, especially with regard to obtaining research assistance, and how do we also ensure that students have the greatest awareness possible of the resources pertinent to their specific needs? How do we do this in such a way that we build their skill sets and confidence and bolster their willingness to persist through graduation? Our position is that a personal librarian program accomplishes these objectives. In addition to building on the kinds of programs and goals that academic librarians have focused on in the past, personal librarian programs also create an exciting opportunity to assist in institutional efforts to keep students on board and get them to successfully complete their specific program of study.

CONCLUSION

Librarians have made tremendous and successful efforts in a wide variety of ways over time to reach students and positively influence learning outcomes. From the traditional provision of reference services librarians have expanded their role to assist through instruction sessions related to enhancing students' information literacy skills, to serve as liaisons to various academic departments, and to be embedded in online courses. They have sought to connect in other ways as well but none perhaps as promising as through personal librarian programs. The intent of a personal librarian program is to build long-term, one-on-one connections that allow students to have the confidence and resources to be successful in the skill sets that librarians particularly seek to instill in them. This book examines some of the first programs of this nature at, among others, Drexel University, Yale University, and Johnson & Wales University's Charlotte campus. Although we make no attempt to cover the concepts comprehensively, we describe information literacy, embedded librarianship, and library liaisonship—and how these successful approaches and initiatives help inform and overlap with a successful personal librarian program or initiative—in detail in later chapters.

Further chapters explore how other services of special libraries and those even outside libraries might creatively inform our approaches in working with students. Certainly, on some basic level libraries have learned from businesses such as Starbucks and Barnes & Noble Booksellers that it is important to create a certain comfort level in terms of the environment. An almost limitless array of new ideas is available to academic librarians if they are willing to be open-minded and consider the possibilities. Librarians should be interested in the ways other businesses and organizations personalize service and how these might be incorporated into personal librarian programs or initiatives. Much can be learned as well from other departments across college and university campuses. Centers for academic support, information technology services, health services, career services, admissions, student financial services, and student affairs are all areas where personalization of services is occurring. The possibility for both learning and partnerships is almost limitless.

Further along we also hear from an experienced faculty member who shares some research on the faculty perspective of a personal librarian program and suggestions for creating and making improvements to such a program. Again, this analysis proceeds not just from the faculty member's own experience with the personal librarian program and literature but also from data he has collected regarding other faculty members' experiences and interpretations.

Best practices are then discussed and explored. The focus in this discussion is not just on what we could do but more so on how we can do it. The intent is to provide the reader with quick and practical ways to get started with a personal librarian program, no matter what size the school or how many library staff are available to assist.

Finally, this book concludes by considering widely and openly the many possibilities for personal librarian programs in the future and assessing the impact that technology may have as we move forward. There is no doubt that we have all experienced a sea change in recent years in libraries, higher education, and the world in general. We firmly believe that personalization of services is the future but that this will manifest itself in many different ways. We don't pretend to be soothsayers but do believe that we have the collective background and experience to make some logical guesses in this regard. We look forward to sharing them with you! So, sit back and enjoy as we share with you some background on Johnson & Wales University's Charlotte campus, its library services, and how a personal librarian program has been developing there. Other key institutions such as Drexel University and Yale University, openly referred to and recognized as the forerunners and pioneers of this new and exciting enterprise, are also explored.

NOTES

1. Spitzer, *Information Literacy*, 13–14.
2. Association of College and Research Libraries, "Presidential Committee on Information Literacy."
3. Association of College and Research Libraries, "Information Literacy Competency Standards."
4. Salony, "History of Bibliographic Instruction," 32.
5. Brendle-Moczuk, "Encouraging Students' Lifelong Learning," 500.
6. Morabito, "Online Distance Education," 24–28.
7. Parker, Lenhart, and Moore, "Digital Revolution and Higher Education."
8. "LMS Market Expected to Triple in the Next 5 Years to $7.8 Billion."
9. Shumaker, *Embedded Librarian*, 5.
10. Drewes and Hoffman, "Academic Embedded Librarianship," 76.
11. Haddow, "Academic Library Use," 132.
12. Nagda et al., "Undergraduate Student–Faculty Research Partnerships," 57.

BIBLIOGRAPHY

Association of College and Research Libraries. "Information Literacy Competency Standards for Higher Education." American Library Association. Last updated January 18, 2000. www.ala.org/acrl/standards/informationliteracycompetency.

Association of College and Research Libraries. "Presidential Committee on Information Literacy: A Final Report." American Library Association. Last updated January 10, 1989. www.ala.org/acrl/publications/whitepapers/presidential.

Brendle-Moczuk, Daniel. "Encouraging Students' Lifelong Learning through Graded Information Literacy Assignments." *Reference Services Review* 34, no. 4 (2006): 498–508.

Drewes, Kathy, and Nadine Hoffman. "Academic Embedded Librarianship: An Introduction." *Public Services Quarterly* 6, no. 2/3 (2010): 75–82.

Haddow, Gaby. "Academic Library Use and Student Retention: A Quantitative Analysis." *Library and Information Science Research* 35 (2013): 127–136.

"LMS Market Expected to Triple in the Next 5 Years to $7.8 Billion." Moodle News. Last updated May 20, 2014. www.moodlenews.com/2013/lms-market-expected -to-triple-in-the-next-5-years-to-7-8-billion.

Morabito, Margaret. "Online Distance Education: Historical and Practical Application." Unpublished diss., American Coastline University, 1997.

Nagda, Biren A., Sandra R. Gregerman, John Jonides, William von Hippel, and Jennifer S. Lerner. "Undergraduate Student–Faculty Research Partnerships Affect Student Retention." *Review of Higher Education* 22, no. 1 (1998): 55–72.

Parker, Kim, Amanda Lenhart, and Kathleen Moore. "The Digital Revolution and Higher Education. " *Pew Research Social and Demographic Trends*, August 28, 2011. www.pewsocialtrends.org/2011/08/28/the-digital-revolution-and-higher -education/3.

Salony, Mary. "The History of Bibliographic Instruction: Changing Trends from Books to the Electronic World." *The Reference Librarian* 24, no. 51 (1995): 31–51.

Shumaker, David. *The Embedded Librarian: Innovative Strategies for Taking Knowledge Where It's Needed*. Medford, NJ: Information Today, 2012.

Spitzer, Kathleen. *Information Literacy: Information Skills for the Information Age*. Syracuse, NY: Clearinghouse on Information and Technology, Syracuse University, 1998.

JEAN MOATS

2

Development and Implementation of the Personal Librarian Concept

APPROACHING A REFERENCE DESK IN A LIBRARY CAN BE A scary proposition, especially for a first-year student who is away from home for the first time. Constance A. Mellon, in her seminal article "Library Anxiety: A Grounded Theory and Its Development," found "that 75 to 85 percent of students in each class described their initial response to the library in terms of fear or anxiety."[1] These students feel overwhelmed with classes and assignments. At the same time, they may wish to see a familiar face amidst all of the strangers or even to have someone to reach out to in order to get information about classes and other campus activities. If contact is not made quickly and information acquired, then students may continue to feel lost academically. A personal touch can provide the support a wandering first-year student needs to stay in school. One way to provide that support may be found in having a personal librarian. In this chapter, we look at the development of the personal librarian concept in several contexts from its beginnings to the present day.

YOUR PATRONS

Who is that first-year student who just walked into your library? The majority of first-year students are eighteen years old and have recently graduated from high school. The typical students may have attended a summer orientation with family members. Now they are on campus, possibly living away from home for the first time and feeling uneasy in this new college environment. Other students are commuting from home to a disorientating and bewildering new environment, dealing with all of the hassles of traffic, parking on campus, and trying to find their classrooms.

An instructor has assigned a research paper and suggested they visit the campus library. When they arrive at the library, the brave ones approach the reference desk to ask for help. Most of the others approach the library's computers and begin to search for information with Google. While these students find information, the results prove unsatisfactory for the instructor and lead to bad grades. The students use the first answer that shows up in Google instead of looking in a library database. What might the outcome be if a first-year student had been assigned a personal librarian? This librarian would be someone the student could contact and ask for help in working on the research paper, including finding information in books and databases. This student has an advantage over his or her peers who are afraid or do not know how to ask for help. By using more credible sources, the student will discover the value of taking the time to do quality research and in turn get a better grade.

Another group of patrons is the adult learners who are coming back to school after being away. Generally, these patrons/students are older in years than traditional students, may be working to support a family, and have been absent from higher education for some time.[2] They may also be apprehensive about returning to the classroom and about asking a librarian for help. Even though these learners seem independent and self-directed, they still want to know that help is available from a librarian.[3] These individuals are perfect candidates for spending time with a personal librarian who offers individual support and attention.

International students can also benefit from being connected to a personal librarian. According to the Institute of International Education, 819,644 foreign students attended U.S. colleges and universities during the 2012–2013 academic year.[4] These students face major challenges, such as language and communication problems, when adjusting to new educational and library systems and general cultural and social environments.[5] Personal librarians can support these students as they settle into their new environment and help them share their culture with the campus community. As a librarian becomes acquainted with the students, he or she may find opportunities for doing displays in the library about students' home countries.

Graduate and doctoral students are also good candidates to benefit from a personal librarian. Institutions struggle with keeping doctoral students until they finish their programs. In "The Case for Partnering Doctoral Students with Librarians: A Synthesis of the Literatures," Colleen S. Harris writes that while students may do fine with the coursework, they are more likely to leave during the research phase. Her article explores how librarians can position themselves to help with this need for improving graduate students' research skills.[6] Personal librarians can assist students at any level of study with research strategies and searches.

A final group of patrons is the faculty and staff at a college or university. Many libraries have liaison librarians assigned to either departments or colleges on campus. Jenna Freedman, who implemented a personal librarian program at Barnard College, writes that their departmental liaison librarians became departmental personal librarians for the faculty.[7] These faculty need to have a personal librarian whom they can contact about library research or instruction sessions for their classes. If the faculty members are more familiar with the resources the library has to offer, then they are more likely to use the librarians in their classes for instruction. Freedman states that this outreach was very successful, as five new faculty members all took advantage of the program.[8]

SAM HOUSTON STATE UNIVERSITY

In 1984, the librarians at Newton Gresham Library at Sam Houston State University began their personal librarian program to assist graduate students. The National Center for Education Statistics' 2010 survey lists the Newton Gresham Library as having 17.50 professional librarians with an FTE total student population of 14,995.[9] The program is at the Newton Gresham Library at Sam Houston State University, a public institution located in Huntsville, Texas. Bill Bailey, reference librarian at Sam Houston State University, writes about their "One to One" program in which graduate students can sign up for a personal librarian. The students who are working on research and writing a thesis complete an application that is signed by their faculty advisor. A reference librarian conducts a personal interview with the graduate student to find out about the topic being researched. Then, the relationship between the student and the librarian begins.[10] Bailey writes that the advantages of this program are its level of formality, because of the application process for the student, and the bigger buy-in by all of the parties involved, because of the faculty advisors' awareness of the librarian's role.[11] This program provides individual support to doctoral students and master's students engaged in thesis research.[12]

CUSHING/WHITNEY MEDICAL LIBRARY
AT YALE UNIVERSITY SCHOOL OF MEDICINE

In 1996, as an outreach initiative, the reference librarians at Cushing/Whitney Medical Library at Yale University School of Medicine started their personal librarian program.[13] They were concerned about their declining contact and face time with the medical students.[14] Since these students had become more comfortable with the computer and the World Wide Web, the librarians wanted to see what changes in format were needed as the digital information environment had evolved. These special librarians wanted to find out about their students' information needs as well as to have the students become more familiar with the library and the librarians themselves.[15] From these ideas, the personal librarian program was born. Judy M. Spak and Janis G. Glover write in their article "The Personal Librarian Program: An Evaluation of a Cushing/Whitney Medical Library Outreach Initiative, "[T]he goals were simple: (1) divide the incoming medical student class evenly among five reference librarians; (2) send three to four messages in one year (so as not to inundate them with too much information); and (3) report anecdotally at the end of the first year."[16] The Education Services Librarian got the roster for the incoming class, divided up the class among the participating librarians, prepared a welcome message for the personal librarians to send, and reminded them to send out other messages throughout the year. This framework was the setup as the program began in the fall of 1996.[17] The librarians keep in contact with the students throughout their medical school careers. This personal librarian program continues to be successful and serves as a model for other schools starting similar programs. In 2006, the librarians conducted a survey to find out if the students were satisfied with the program and to identify what improvements might be made. Overall, the students were pleased with the program and gave examples of how their personal librarians had helped them with research.[18]

UNIVERSITY OF RICHMOND

In the fall of 2000, Boatwright Library at the University of Richmond started a personal librarian program for freshman students. The National Center for Education Statistics' 2010 survey lists Boatwright Library as having 18.75 full-time librarians with an FTE total student population of 4,015.[19] Lucretia McCulley, director of outreach services at the library, had a personal banker at the time who was available to answer her questions. She decided to apply the same idea to the library for first-year students. McCulley thought a personal librarian would be a great way to reach out to them. In the first version of the program, eleven liaison librarians divided up the first-year students. Each librarian ended up with about eighty students. Then, the librarians sent out letters with their business cards in them to each student.[20]

The personal librarians could make personal connections with the students and let them know about library resources.[21] The program continues today with each first-year student class attending the University of Richmond. McCulley remarks that a trademark of a student's time at the University of Richmond is the personal connection made with librarians.[22]

YALE UNIVERSITY

The personal librarian program at Yale University Library started in 2008. Emily Horning and Sue Roberts based the program on the one at Cushing/Whitney Medical Library mentioned earlier in this chapter.[23] They planned to adapt materials used in a small program to a larger population.

Yale University has three major academic components: Yale College, for undergraduate students; the Graduate School of Arts and Sciences; and the professional schools.[24] Nineteen branch libraries comprise the university library system. The National Center for Education Statistics' 2010 survey lists 168 full-time librarians with an FTE student population of 11,559.[25] One can understand Horning and Roberts's hesitation, as their program was to provide research assistance to the entire freshman class of 1,000 students when it began in 2008.[26] The program had been successful in the medical library because of the smaller number of students. Yet, Horning and Roberts moved forward with the project partly in response to the librarians' perceptions of having lost contact with students as more resources moved online.[27]

In the fall of 2012, 1,356 first-year students entered Yale.[28] On Yale's personal librarian program webpage, 33 librarians are listed as personal librarians. The program "is designed to introduce students entering Yale College to the collections and services of Yale University Library."[29] Students are matched with a personal librarian for their freshman and sophomore years. Then, they move on to a subject specialist once they have declared a major.[30] Subjects covered by the specialists include anthropology, psychology, religious studies, medical studies, and international relations.[31] Today, many libraries use Yale's program as an example when seeking to implement a personal librarian program.[32]

DREXEL UNIVERSITY

In 2010, Drexel University started its personal librarian program for entering freshman students, providing guidance and a link to the library services. The National Center for Education Statistics' 2010 survey lists Drexel as having a main library, two branch libraries, and twenty-five full-time librarians for a total FTE student enrollment of 18,754.[33] Danuta A. Nitecki, Dean of Libraries, brought the idea for this program to Drexel from her previous position at Yale University Library.[34] She had seen the success of the program and decided to implement it at Drexel. In 2010, more than twenty librarians participated in the program, with each being assigned to a group of at least 100 students.[35]

The personal librarians contact the first-year students before they start classes. Throughout the semester, the librarians e-mail students information about research resources, encouraging the students to make use of them.[36] Personal librarians also help connect students with campus resources, making the transition to college a little easier. Their areas of responsibility include navigating the library environment, providing information about research tools, connecting students to the right person, and letting students know about upcoming library events and/or new resources.[37]

By offering these services, the library hopes to add a more personal element to the student experience. The students are encouraged to contact their personal librarians when seeking credible information for assignments. The personal librarians will maintain these relationships with students until the students are more involved with their academic majors. At that point, the students' primary contact becomes a subject specialist who may also serve as a liaison to Drexel's colleges and schools.[38] In many ways, liaisons are extensions of personal librarians.

JOHNSON & WALES UNIVERSITY

The personal librarian program at Johnson & Wales University in Charlotte, North Carolina, came about from the library staff's desire to become better acquainted with the students. The librarians already had a great working relationship with the majority of the faculty members. They wanted to build on those relationships to provide better services to the students. One of the librarians wanted to have a better understanding of the material being taught in a Culture and Food class. She arranged to be embedded in this class during fall 2010 and winter 2010–2011 terms. In this situation, embedded meant attending each class session and assisting the instructor with preparing the class syllabus. The librarian contributed resources that were used in the class discussions and activities. This setup worked well for both the instructor and the librarian. By attending every class session and helping design the assignments, the librarian was able to get to know the students better in class, and this carried over to more personalized contact in the library. The students benefited from the extra assistance in the class and in the library.

During the fall term of the 2011–2012 academic year, the university administration formed several committees on campus to look at retention issues. These committees were charged with coming up with ideas and programs to help keep students in school to finish their degrees. A librarian volunteered to be on the Culinary/Arts and Sciences Retention Team, which included faculty, staff, and students. One of the ideas suggested under building connections and easing transitions for students was a personal librarian program. Some of the team members had seen examples of this program on the Yale University Library and Barnard College Library websites. After discussing the program with the rest of the library staff, the librarian returned to the retention team, making a commitment that the library would implement the program with the first-year students entering the school in September 2012. Johnson & Wales University enrolled 758 students that year.

The proposed framework was to assign the four full-time librarians to the ENG 1020 (English Composition) instructors. Each first-year student is required to take ENG 1020, a beginning writing and composition class, at some point. Each class would come to the library for information literacy–related instruction, which would be taught by the librarian assigned to that class, if possible. The assigned librarian would explain the personal librarian program to the class. The librarians would be connected to the course management system, ulearn, as a way to stay informed about the course assignments. The ulearn system also allowed and continues to allow the librarians to contact the students by e-mail for that particular class. E-mails were sent to the students throughout the term, informing them about new library resources and offering help on assignments for not only ENG 1020 but also any other classes the student was enrolled in that term. Some of the librarians visited the ENG 1020 classes before providing information literacy instruction.

At the beginning of each term, the librarians were assigned again to the ENG 1020 instructors and new classes of students. The librarians continued to e-mail their students from previous terms. The librarians also shared information about the personal librarian program through a video made during the faculty orientation at the beginning of the year. The librarians attended the English instructors' departmental meeting to address any concerns from the faculty. The librarians also contacted their assigned instructors to introduce themselves. As word spread about the personal librarian program, faculty members from other departments requested personal librarians for their classes. By the end of the first year, the librarians had been involved in thirty-seven individual classes. Chapter 8 explores in greater detail faculty reaction to the initiative as well as student impact as it relates to student work and learning.

IMPLEMENTATION OF PERSONAL LIBRARIAN PROGRAMS

A sampling of the websites accompanying personal librarian programs reveals a number of similarities in the services being offered. The common goal of most programs is to introduce new students to the library and library services. As mentioned earlier, many schools follow Yale's example in listing how personal librarians can help students. Here is a sample from Yale:

Your PL will:

- Keep you informed with periodic e-mail messages highlighting new resources and programs especially for students, as well as notices and timely reminders, such as extended Library hours during Reading Week and finals
- Answer your questions about Library policies, procedures and services, such as RefWorks workshops and Borrow Direct
- Assist with finding information for your research assignments, by helping you articulate your research question, identify the best sources and formulate your search strategy
- Support you even when you're not around (on vacation, or away from Yale doing research)
- Help you when you don't know where to start, or you can't think of what to do next[39]

How do institutions assign students to a personal librarian? Many of the larger schools randomly assign first-year and second-year students to the librarians. Some programs assign students alphabetically or based on residence hall floors or learning communities. Others use first-year class rosters to divide up the students or assign librarians to core courses like English, giving each librarian specific instructors and their classes. Personal librarian programs with graduate students often require the students to fill out and submit an application to the library. These applications also need the signature of the faculty advisor. Several websites also have search boxes students can use to find out who their librarian is.

Once a student declares a major, the student may be reassigned to a subject specialist or to a liaison, depending on the program's guidelines. The purpose is to provide students with a specialist more familiar with a particular subject and its specific resources. One challenge might be that the librarians end up not wanting to pass on their students to a subject specialist. For example, one student saved an e-mail received years earlier from a librarian. This student knew that one day this librarian's assistance would be needed in doing research.[40]

In essence, personal librarians keep their students informed about resources and programs through periodic e-mails. They answer questions about library policies and procedures, assist with research strategies for projects, connect students with subject specialists, and support students when they are away from campus. Students are encouraged to meet in person with their assigned librarian. Personal librarians serve as a point of contact for students.

LIBRARIANS' REACTIONS TO THE PROGRAM

Librarians have positive reactions to participating in personal librarian programs. They see such programs as another way of demystifying the library and helping the students to have a better experience.[41] At the Cushing/Whitney Medical Library, the librarians in the program are enthusiastic about their participation.[42] At some libraries, the rate of participation among students was low in the early stages. However, in their later years in school and as more research projects were assigned, more students began to take advantage of the resources the personal librarians offered.

At the University of Richmond, Lucretia McCulley tells about seniors who came by the library after rediscovering the letter they had received from their personal librarian. As they reread the letter, these seniors remembered what a great idea this outreach program had been for them.[43]

As libraries explore starting a personal librarian program, there is a concern about how much extra work the staff will be expected to perform. According to the literature, most personal librarians have not seen an increase in their workload. The librarians need to be committed, staying on top of the communication and relationship aspects. Depending on how receptive the students are to the program, the workload may increase slightly for the librarians. However, the advantages for the students that the program provides outweigh any possible negative effects that the library staff might feel.

CONCLUSION

Going away to college can be a scary experience for some first-year students. Everything is new and different, from roommates to challenging academic assignments. It helps to make personal connections. Librarians can reach out to these students and offer to be there for them as they navigate the library and work on class assignments. They can offer that personal touch as personal librarians, possibly helping to keep students in school. As seen in the models described, a personal librarian program is not just for small or private schools. It can be implemented at just about any institution. However, factors such as majors, numbers of students, and numbers of available librarians are all important considerations when crafting a program that will work at your institution. In that regard, this book is intended to act as a guide for you.

NOTES

1. Mellon, "Library Anxiety," 162.
2. Ismail, "Getting Personal," 246.
3. Ibid., 248.
4. Institute of International Education, "International Student Enrollment Trends."
5. Baron and Strout-Dapaz, "Communicating with and Empowering International Students," 314.
6. Harris, "Case for Partnering," 599.
7. Freedman, "Implementing a Personal Librarian Program," 12.
8. Ibid.
9. Institute of Education Statistics, "Search for Schools and Colleges."
10. Bailey, "Personal Librarian," 1820.
11. Ibid., 1821.
12. Newton Gresham Library, "One to One."
13. Spak and Glover, "Personal Librarian Program," 16.
14. Ibid.
15. Ibid.
16. Ibid.
17. Ibid.
18. Ibid., 24.
19. Institute of Education Statistics, "Search for Schools and Colleges."
20. Dillon, "Personal Librarian Program," 11.
21. Ibid.
22. Ibid.
23. Tidmarsh, "Slight Rise in Use."
24. "Academic Programs > Schools."
25. Institute of Education Statistics, "Search for Schools and Colleges."
26. Tidmarsh, "Slight Rise in Use."
27. Ibid.
28. Office of Institutional Research, "Yale 'Factsheet.'"
29. Horning, "Personal Librarian Program."
30. Ibid.
31. "Subject Specialists."
32. Oder and Blumenstein, "Newsdesk," 14.
33. Institute of Education Statistics, "Search for Schools and Colleges."

34. Ibid.
35. Ibid.
36. "Personal Librarian for Every Drexel Freshman."
37. Bellafante, "My Personal Librarian."
38. "Personal Librarian for Every Drexel Freshman."
39. Horning, "Personal Librarian Program."
40. Nann, "Personal Librarians," 22.
41. Kolowich, "Libraries Make It Personal."
42. Spak and Glover, "Personal Librarian Program," 24.
43. Dillon, "Personal Librarian Program," 12.

BIBLIOGRAPHY

"Academic Programs > Schools." Yale University. Accessed June 14, 2013. www.yale
    .edu/schools/index.html.

Bailey, Bill. "The Personal Librarian." *Library Journal* 109, no. 16 (1984): 1820–1821.

Baron, Sara, and Alexia Strout-Dapaz. "Communicating with and Empowering
    International Students with a Library Skills Set." *Reference Services Review* 29,
    no. 4 (2001): 314–326.

Bellafante, Nancy. "My Personal Librarian." Drexel University Libraries. Last updated
    October 2, 2013. www.library.drexel.edu/personal-librarian.

Dillon, Cy. "The Personal Librarian Program at the University of Richmond: An
    Interview with Lucretia McCulley." *Virginia Libraries* 57, no. 3 (2011): 11–12.

Freedman, Jenna. "Implementing a Personal Librarian Program for Students and
    Faculty at Barnard College." *The Unabashed Librarian* 157 (2011): 11–13.

Harris, Colleen S. "The Case for Partnering Doctoral Students with Librarians: A
    Synthesis of the Literatures." *Library Review* 60, no. 7 (2011): 599–620.

Horning, Emily. "Personal Librarian Program." Yale University Library. Last modified
    March 26, 2013. www.library.yale.edu/pl.

Institute of Education Statistics. "Search for Schools and Colleges." National
    Center for Education Statistics. Accessed June 13, 2013. http://nces.ed.gov/
    globallocator.

Institute of International Education. "International Student Enrollment Trends,
    1949/50–2012/13." Open Doors Report on International Educational Exchange,
    2013. www.iie.org/Research-and-Publications/Open-Doors/Data/International
    -Students/Enrollment-Trends/1948-2012.

Ismail, Lizah. "Getting Personal: Reaching Out to Adult Learners through a Course
    Management System." *The Reference Librarian* 52 (2011): 244–262.

Kolowich, Steve. "Libraries Make It Personal." *Inside Higher Ed*, September 28, 2010.
    www.insidehighered.com/news/2010/09/28/librarians.

Mellon, Constance A. "Library Anxiety: A Grounded Theory and Its Development." *College and Research Libraries* 47 (1986): 160–165.

Nann, John B. "Personal Librarians." *AALL Spectrum* 14, no. 8 (2010): 20–23.

Newton Gresham Library. "One to One." Sam Houston State University. Accessed June 16, 2013. http://library.shsu.edu/services/onetoone.

Oder, Norman, and Lynn Blumenstein. "Newsdesk: Personal Librarian Program at Drexel University." *Library Journal* 109, no. 16 (2010): 14.

Office of Institutional Research. "Yale 'Factsheet.'" Yale University. Last updated March 21, 2014. http://oir.yale.edu/yale-factsheet.

"Personal Librarian for Every Drexel Freshman." DrexelNOW. September 3, 2010. www.drexel.edu/now/news-media/releases/archive/2010/September/A-Personal-Librarian-For-Every-Drexel-Freshman.

Spak, Judy M., and Janis G. Glover. "The Personal Librarian Program: An Evaluation of a Cushing/Whitney Medical Library Outreach Initiative." *Medical References Services Quarterly* 26, no. 4 (2007): 15–25.

"Subject Specialists." Yale University Library. Last modified June 20, 2011. http://resources.library.yale.edu/StaffDirectory/subjects.aspx.

Tidmarsh, David. "Slight Rise in Use of Personal Librarians." *Yale Daily News*, November 11, 2009. http://yaledailynews.com/blog/2009/11/11/slight-rise-in-use-of-personal-librarians.

JOE ESHLEMAN

3
Information Literacy
and the Personal Librarian

LITTLE HAS BEEN WRITTEN IN DETAIL ON THE CONNECTION
between library instruction and personal librarian programs. From a marketing point of view, most personal librarian programs do not specifically target library instruction or information literacy initiatives as part of their focus. That is not to say that information literacy does not play a role in personal librarian programs. In fact, many of the major tenets of information literacy drive the core objectives of library programs that focus on individual research help. Because students could be said to be under pressure from various responsibilities, uninterested due to numerous distractions, and possibly unable to understand the research process and requirements, offering a helping and welcoming hand in the library instruction classroom and reinforcing the importance of developing a sustained connection with a librarian can be of utmost importance.[1]

THE DEVELOPMENT OF INFORMATION LITERACY

Because a significant number of college and university libraries with library instruction programs use information literacy concepts and standards as a baseline for constructing their sessions and classes, it is valuable to lay out a background before considering how information literacy and personal librarian programs interact. In the author's experience, the majority of students are not aware of the foundations of information literacy, and few make the effort to learn about the subject. Interestingly enough, this lack of knowledge about the term does not hinder the ability to grasp its core concepts. Despite the absence of general knowledge that students have about information literacy, it is germane to the personal librarian conversation to have some understanding of its historic context, current use, and future direction.

The term *information literacy* was first used in 1974 in a proposal submitted by Paul Zurkowski, then president of the U.S. Information Industry Association.[2] As time went on, the term became connected to the library field in conjunction with earlier forms of library instruction (typically referred to as *bibliographic instruction*), and information literacy concepts continued to make strides in education circles. In 2000, the Association of College and Research Libraries (ACRL) approved the "Information Literacy Competency Standards for Higher Education":

> STANDARD ONE: The information literate student determines the nature and extent of the information needed. . . .
>
> STANDARD TWO: The information literate student accesses needed information effectively and efficiently. . . .
>
> STANDARD THREE: The information literate student evaluates information and its sources critically and incorporates selected information into his or her knowledge base and value system. . . .
>
> STANDARD FOUR: The information literate student, individually or as a member of a group, uses information effectively to accomplish a specific purpose. . . .
>
> STANDARD FIVE: The information literate student understands many of the economic, legal, and social issues surrounding the use of information and accesses and uses information ethically and legally. . . .[3]

In sum, these Standards encompass the self-reflective and purposeful process of knowing when an information need occurs, having the skills to find information, assessing the quality of the information, and using it in a responsible manner.

Certainly before the year 2000 and the adoption of these Standards similar conceptual ideas and guidelines about one's relationship with information existed. In the framework of the library, a comprehensive source for material about the history of libraries that led to the adoption of information literacy is Donna L. Gilton's "Information Literacy Instruction: A History in Context."[4] Gilton ties in historical and societal factors that contributed to the changes in the library's approach to its primary role and sifts through the library chronology that paved the way for the concept of information literacy. Information literacy adoption was a direct response to technology changes, and, as such, the Standards can appear to wrestle with continual change. The consistent view of libraries as entities that help their constituents with information and research needs led to the desire for some type of concrete criteria and a singular banner under which those needs are assessed. The majority of academic libraries, following ACRL's lead, have adopted the Standards and use them in some capacity in relation to library instruction.

A quick demarcation is in order here. In some respect, *library instruction* can be used as an umbrella term for the structured sessions that occur in an academic library to help students understand basic use of library resources and procedures and to promote lifelong research skills. The sessions can also offer the opportunity to introduce librarians. Nicole A. Cooke elaborates: "Library instruction is simply explained as a scheduled session where a librarian systematically instructs learners on how to successfully and efficiently manipulate the library's information resources."[5] Information literacy can be thought of as the theoretical bedrock and foundation for learning outcome goals upon which most library instruction is based. To put it another way, information literacy tenets are taught during library instruction, yet the skills can be used anywhere. ACRL provides a starting point with overviews, resources, guides, and programs for further exploration of information literacy on its information literacy–targeted website (www.ala.org/acrl/issues/infolit).[6]

The ACRL Standards, as mentioned previously, were written in 2000. There are plans to revise them due to the changing nature of our world. As the technologies we use to interact with ever-changing devices, the systems we create to access information, and the information needs and resources themselves are in continual flux, standards are subject to revision. One aspect of this change involves moving away from honing basic information use skill sets to gaining an even deeper understanding of one's relationship to information and moving toward knowledge creation. Being information literate will continue to be a moving target, and, similar to lifelong learning, one will constantly need to work/update/reinvent to be proficient when doing research. This situation results in present and future needs for information literacy instruction and, often in conjunction with, personal librarian programs.

Information literacy and library instruction go hand in hand in most academic libraries. As information literacy gained in stature and became more widespread as a general learning outcome on campuses, it moved outward from the library. Although library instruction in an academic library often takes place in a computer lab or a classroom, there are also opportunities at the reference desk and within face-to-face meetings to teach students about the library and the librarians and to create a personalized connection.

THE REFERENCE DESK AND
ONE-ON-ONE APPOINTMENTS

In some ways, the model of the reference interview can be considered as akin to a personal information literacy session. The one-on-one conversations and the time spent with students at the reference desk are often referred to as *reference transactions*. The personal librarian concept stresses relations over transactions and therefore attempts to "elongate" aspects of the reference desk interview. David Shumaker and Mary Talley, proponents of embedded librarianship, use the terms *transactional* and *relational* to differentiate between the rudimentary and ephemeral research needs that sometimes occur at the reference desk and the more involved and consistent connections that can happen within embedded situations.[7] The ability for a student to schedule an appointment with a librarian to attain some research help is so prevalent in academic libraries that it could be considered to be an answer to the question, "Why would you *not* implement a personal librarian program at your library?" The answer in many academic library cases is, "We have no need to because we are already doing all of the things that a personal librarian program does." That is to say that a number of academic libraries consider it redundant or a simple marketing ploy to create this type of program. Yet perhaps it is not quite that simple. Our purpose here is to differentiate some of the widespread roles of the librarian (reference, instruction) from basic implementation to a more focused, persistent, and personalized motive.

Andy Woodworth, who blogs at *Agnostic, Maybe*, offers five reasons why one-on-one appointments should be implemented in libraries. Three of these include that time (and staffing) are well spent, the number of computer-related topics that require instruction have increased, and the ability to create personal, tailored sessions exists. In reference to a personal or tailored session, Woodworth adds that "it puts a staff member in a more casual context with the patron where they can open up about the topic. Unlike the group setting, people will be more frank about their questions or issues in the one-on-one setting. This further deepens the connection and allows me to teach towards their strengths and issues."[8] Here we see how the one-on-one setting allows for more focused personalization.

Sometimes one-on-one sessions with students take the form of "make-up" meetings wherein the student was absent for a library instruction class and is making the effort to meet with the instruction librarian to find out more about the missed information. Adrian Pauw from Gonzaga University's Foley Center Library discusses the pros and cons of one-on-one meetings and finds that positives occur, such as tailoring an appointment to an individual's research needs in a timely and relevant manner and learning from students about how they go about their research and what resources the library might be lacking. Most important, "We forge positive long-term relationships with library patrons."[9]

More parallels to the focus of the one-on-one appointment can be found in other university services and the student-directed approaches that those services use that closely mimic a personal librarian program. Some libraries have found that as a personal librarian program gains momentum, the time required to provide assistance at the reference desk is minimized, and sometimes the desk disappears completely in favor of more individual librarian–student appointment times. Departments such as centers for academic support generally schedule individual time with tutors, so a parallel can be seen here as well.

Amanda Hovious, who blogs at *Designer Librarian*, suggests in her post "The Key to Information Literacy? Help-Seeking" that "classroom instructors require students to meet one-on-one with a librarian (preferably more) during a semester course."[10] Although this appears to be a sound proposition, some librarians, students, and faculty may feel trepidation when it comes to mandatory requirements and the library. Reducing library anxiety is one objective of a personal librarian relationship, and forcing a get-together could undermine a potentially natural course of events where the student takes the initiative to meet with the librarian. An approach that combines library instruction and the opportunity for scheduling one-on-one appointments can expand students' options as well as lessen their feelings of pressure and anxiety. How students view information literacy, library instruction, and librarians and how these ideas impact students are explored in the next two sections. The importance of focusing on user needs and on relationship building in the library is also discussed.

INFORMATION LITERACY INSTRUCTION AND STUDENTS

In her survey of tactics for librarians to keep pace with the continual changes in their field, Nicole A. Cooke walks through some of the ways in which libraries have refocused their priorities. She points out that Brenda Dervin observed in 1977 that libraries need "to rethink and restructure their services based on need of their users, and not rest on the laurels of prior successes, or overestimate the inherent value of libraries because they possess desired information . . . [because] there is an 'increasing demand by users of systems that they be treated as individuals.'" Dervin surmises, "To this end, libraries must strive to create 'activities that are communication-based rather than simply information-based.'"[11] This summary, focusing on individual need and connections, is a fine way to define core personal librarian goals as they relate to library instruction.

Personal librarian programs generally target first-year students and occasionally add second-year students as well. Some programs also aim for transfer students or international students as a main audience. One of the desired outcomes of personal librarian programs regardless of the audience or the naming of the program is, of course, to help students understand the research process and guide them through whatever hurdles they may encounter when searching for information for their assignments. As mentioned earlier, despite the case that many first-year students are not familiar with the tenets of information literacy, much less with the phrase itself and what it means, it is important for them to be taught of its underpinnings so that an understanding of the concepts can take hold. Many institutions that offer for-credit information literacy courses focus more closely on teaching the aforementioned ACRL Standards.

The relationship-building opportunity that can occur during a library instruction session is obvious and yet is not always a priority. One way to address this missed chance comes with the realization that there are numerous types of students and, therefore, several entry points into the library. When we consider the myriad preconceived notions and past experiences that inform how students think about both the library and the librarians, we can begin to see how librarians can function as bridges between students and libraries. In volume 50, issue 1, of *Reference Librarian*, the overarching topic is "Serving Underserved Populations," and numerous articles single out overlooked student groups. The author of the introduction to the volume finds that "aggressive outreach is critical when dealing with the underserved." The article as a whole points out ways in which to consider and engage "several often-underserved groups—minority students, the visually impaired, the homeless, the young, and the aged—who face a variety of barriers in both academic and public library settings."[12] Certainly it is not a far-fetched notion that all students can benefit from a more proactive and personal approach by an instruction librarian, which points out that the main librarian role is one of continuing active participation and dedicated service.

How students see librarians has become a crucial issue, not only in the library instruction classroom, but also in all other library interactions. The Ethnographic Research in Illinois Academic Libraries (ERIAL) Project was a twenty-one-month research study conducted in 2008–2010 that investigated how students conduct research and use library resources and services. In the book *College Libraries and Student Culture: What We Now Know*, which is based on the findings of this study, Annie Armstrong states that faculty believe "librarians should emphasize their role not only as experts in research, but as mentors and encouragers of students, both within and outside the classroom."[13] In their chapter titled "Why Don't Students Ask Librarians for Help? Undergraduate Help-Seeking Behavior in Three Academic Libraries," Susan Miller and Nancy Murillo relate, "Students may not seek help from librarians in part because our universities do not ensure that our students and librarians connect with each other. Library instruction may not be required for students."[14] They conclude:

> Students will seek help from those with whom they have established relationships. . . . Relationships with librarians can start early in students' college years and build over time. With institutional support, librarians can foster these kinds of relationships via peer mentor programs, graded library assignments that emerge from librarian–faculty collaborations, and increased librarian outreach efforts to meet students in-person and online. In this way, librarians position themselves to work with other departments, programs, and campus initiatives so that seeking help from librarians is not only encouraged, but essential.[15]

Once again, the importance of relationship building is at the forefront of approaches to helping students with their research on a consistent basis. During the 2011 American College and Research Libraries Conference, ERIAL presented a poster with strategies that librarians can use to improve relationships with students:

- Librarians can place more instructional emphasis on all types of information sources rather than merely library sources, e.g., discussion of Wikipedia in library classes.
- Outreach to faculty can focus on disciplinary goals to make library instruction more relevant, e.g., teach the structure of the literature review, not just finding articles.
- Integrated strategies can address information literacy shortfalls, e.g., student assessment, including an information literacy in college orientation course.[16]

The ERIAL study takes many of the perspectives of the library and librarians that both faculty and students have and views them from social and anthropological points of view. This approach, which primarily focuses on firsthand accounts, relationships, roles, and needs, ties in well with personal librarian objectives. Two conclusions of the research are that "the invisibility of librarians within the academic lives of students was also a recurring theme"[17] and that "a central cause underlying this lack of use is that students do not have sufficient opportunity to build relationships with librarians, instead relying on the advice of their professors and their peers."[18]

Perhaps moving toward developing the opportunities for librarians and students to meet should be a stronger goal in libraries. In their article "One-Shot or Embedded? Assessing Different Delivery Timing for Information Resources Relevant to Assignments," Amy Van Epps and Megan Sapp Nelson show how a number of short library instruction sessions sprinkled throughout a term benefited the students more than just one meeting. Although the study is presented as preliminary and requiring further investigation, the authors conclude, "More frequent and timely interaction between students and library instruction increases the quality of sources used and the completeness of the citations written."[19] Again, the value of forming a consistent bond can work in an embedded situation or as part of a personal librarian program.

At Johnson & Wales University, a student survey was given in November 2012 after the first term during which the personal librarian program was implemented and forty-four students responded. One of the three questions posed was, "In what ways did the personal librarian program help you with your research this term?" One answer points to how student–librarian relationships can develop:

> I didn't actually contact my personal librarian; however, I went to the library multiple times and asked the librarians on staff at that particular time for help. Most of the time I asked for assistance finding a book on a certain topic. Although I didn't use my personal librarian this term, I think having a librarian is a great idea. I think sometimes students are intimidated by going to their teacher for help and a librarian is a safe person to go to.

It is interesting here to see the contrast between the ideas of the ERIAL study and this particular firsthand experience. Perhaps the best solution to alleviating some of the anxiety that students feel when it comes to assignment and research requirements is through a combination of trusted sources and continuing connections. A fair number of authors of library instruction literature will define (or redefine) information literacy early in an article and then separate their conception from others' by explaining a unique approach or presenting a derivative teaching method. A library instruction approach that prioritizes presenting the core tenets of a personal librarian program (communication, connection, relationship building) as a learning outcome to students can go a long way toward developing a link between these two aspects of librarianship.

INFORMATION LITERACY INSTRUCTION AND PERSONAL LIBRARIAN PROGRAMS

The importance of instruction continues to be acknowledged in the academic library. In essence, the basic goal of a personal librarian program is generally linked to instructing students about the library and the research process. In fact, aspects of a personal librarian program could be considered a more direct, singular, and purposeful flavor of library instruction. One of the reasons that a personal librarian program works so well in conjunction with library instruction is that a given instruction session may be the first in a library for a student. With that noted, it can be advantageous to the student to be introduced to the concept of *the librarian* as *the* primary research resource rather than the physical and virtual library resources. Because relationship building is at the core of any personal librarian program, this puts even more weight on the library instruction interaction in whatever form that may take.

Some of the structure of the "one-shot" library instruction session can be lengthened or amplified by a strong personal librarian program. A brief detour to review aspects of the format and design of library instruction may be helpful here. Terms such as *one-shot instruction session* and *fifty-minute session* describe single-session classroom library instruction as opposed to the librarian interacting with the class over an entire term. This type of library instruction is currently under scrutiny because of the increasing need to reach into the online learning environment. There has also been some recent questioning of its effectiveness. "Full course" classes focused on information literacy, the growing popularity of embedded librarians, and the increasing provision of self-paced information literacy tutorials have led some instruction librarians to rethink the one-shot format. Coming full circle, another way to possibly move away from one-shot sessions is implementing and integrating a robust personal librarian program to revitalize a library instruction program.

To some extent, all instruction is based on the idea of handing off knowledge and skills; an additional goal is boosting the students' confidence to apply the transferred tools. Library anxiety is a well-documented fear that students experience, as already noted. Heather Carlile posits that this fear impacts students' use of the library and their ability to approach librarians for help, that library anxiety "offers an explanation, proposing that a fear of being in and using libraries serves as a psychological barrier, hindering many university students from using the library efficiently and effectively."[20] This quote from a student shows how strong this feeling can be: "'If I was a librarian myself,' said another interviewee, 'the number-one thing I would do is to bring trust to the student. . . . If I was a shy student I wouldn't want to work with a librarian I didn't trust.'"[21]

One of the ways to alleviate this dread is to be approachable and create a welcoming environment in the library instruction classroom. This includes speaking to students respectfully and assuring them that they will be met with an open and helpful attitude. With this in mind, instructors should introduce the goals of a personal librarian program and stress their desire to help the students with their research. Once students are able to gain assurance and confidence, there is a greater chance that they will be able to work with librarians. Initiating and fostering relationships are core goals of personal librarian programs, and library instruction is an optimal place to achieve these markers.

Library instruction can be a strong component of a personal librarian program, although it may not always be presented specifically in promotional material. Most libraries that promote their personal librarian programs on their websites do not mention library instruction as a specific component. One design of a personal librarian program, such as the one at Emory University, is designating librarians to faculty, which parallels the liaison program elsewhere.[22] A responsibility in this type of pairing is to help schedule library instruction sessions for classes.

In the more commonly constructed personal librarian programs, the personal librarian assigned to a class section teaches the library instruction for it and reinforces the personal connection. The structure of the personal librarian program at Johnson & Wales University is anchored by its connection to instruction. In that case, the librarians take the opportunity to introduce both themselves and the details of the program during an introductory session. This format allows the librarians to connect with the students, introduce themselves as "your personal librarian," and point out how they will contact the students throughout the term. It is easy to see how this could potentially alleviate library anxiety as well as reinforce in detail how the librarian can help the student.

If the desire is to integrate a personal librarian program, one excellent opportunity is pairing with library instruction. Depending on the design of library instruction at your institution, introducing yourself as a personal librarian in a classroom setting can reinforce the commitment to the personal librarian ideals. In many cases, the core academic goals of a personal librarian program amount to helping students find credible information for their research assignments, formulating their research questions, helping students choose engaging topics, helping with search strategy, and guiding students when they are citing. One other element that is seen often is proactive communication from the personal librarian to the students throughout the term, generally offering help through e-mail correspondence.

A unique opportunity for librarians can occur within the library instruction format where the instruction librarian is given a forum for promoting relationships in addition to resources. Library literature is replete with calls to extend the fifty-minute session from a "show and tell" layout presenting the library catalog and databases to more active engagement or perhaps relaying the aforementioned ACRL Standards and impressing upon students the value of lifelong learning. One avenue that seems to be overlooked, however, is presenting the librarian as a resource and developing library instruction sessions that market how the student–librarian affiliation can be developed and be beneficial to students. Brent Nunn and Elizabeth Ruane point out how vital, if somewhat difficult, it is to market services and succinctly describe the importance of this to students:

> Imagine if they knew at the beginning of the semester that there were librarians with expertise on their assignments? That librarians could

help them finish their projects more quickly and with better results? The message that should be conveyed to users is: It is not that you (as a savvy Web searcher) cannot find an answer on your own, but that our reference librarians will help you find a better answer, faster. This will mean it will be essential to make reference services feel personalized by linking users with not just a building, but with a face: for-profit companies have effectively demonstrated the impact of having a credible spokesperson to convey the quality of their service, and this technique can work for libraries as well. The end goal of this type of marketing is getting the patron in the door, although not necessarily promising that a particular librarian will be available at the reference desk.[23]

There are two significant points to be made here in relation to the personal librarian ethos. Again, although we see the reference desk as the point of contact, that place does not necessarily need to be where these ideas are promulgated. Also, the last line of the quote highlights one of the reasons that personal librarian programs are not more widespread. That is, some students might be confused about who "their" personal librarian is. In fact, this issue created some problems at our institution until we realized that the concept is larger than the individual. To clarify, although it is important to designate each personal librarian to a particular student, the idea that any librarian will spend quality time helping any student outweighs semantic particulars.

One large aspect of marketing a personal librarian program is blanketed emphasis of the word *personal* in all library materials. For example, the Howard E. Barth Learning Resources Center and the William F. White, Jr. Library at Del Mar College in Corpus Christi, Texas, use "Personal Library Instruction Session."[24] The University of Texas–Dallas Eugene McDermott Library uses the same phrase in its Frequently Asked Questions about library instruction.[25] Although this can be viewed simply as a version of branding a one-on-one appointment with a librarian, some consideration should be given to presentation. One idea is that just using the term *personal* creates a positive, connection-focused atmosphere for faculty and students. Although this can appear to be trite, it has been the author's experience as part of a personal librarian program that faculty enjoy using this term, adhere to its concepts, and appear to take to the program with greater enthusiasm and promulgation than when working with terms such as *information literacy* and *embedded librarian*. An interesting and compelling case can be made that the phrase *personal librarian* has more credence and is more easily identifiable to students than *information literacy*.

The binding element of library instruction and personal librarian programs is self-evident and yet is not always capitalized upon. Using instruction as a platform to introduce and publicize a personal librarian program is a natural fit and offers an excellent forum to initialize relationships.

CONCLUSION

An ongoing thread in this chapter is offering students options to alleviate library trepidation and research anxiety. If the personal librarian philosophy takes hold on a campus and librarians are able to convey who they are and what they do, then perhaps some students' anxiety will be alleviated and the value of the librarian as resource will be seen. The forum in which these ideas are dispersed, whether at the reference desk, in a library instruction class, or during a one-on-one appointment, is not as important as the realization by librarians that actively and consistently supporting students and forming connections with them are of the utmost significance.

NOTES

1. Stephens, "Why Students Plagiarize."
2. Department of Information and Communications, "LearnHigher CETL."
3. Association of College and Research Libraries, "Information Literacy Competency Standards."
4. Gilton, "Information Literacy Instruction."
5. Cooke, "Becoming an Andragogical Librarian," 210.
6. Association of College and Research Libraries, "Information Literacy Competency Standards."
7. Shumaker and Talley, "Models of Embedded Librarianship," 9.
8. Woodworth, "Why Your Library Should Do One-on-One Appointments."
9. Kappus, Jenks, and Pauw, "'Can You Meet with Me on Friday?,'" 8.
10. Hovious, "The Key to Information Literacy?"
11. Cooke, "Professional Development 2.0," 2–3, 3.
12. Miller, "Introduction: Serving Underserved Populations," 1.
13. Armstrong, "Marketing the Library's Instructional Services," 37.
14. Miller and Murillo, "Why Don't Students Ask?," 60.
15. Ibid., 69–70.
16. Asher et al., "Feeling Like a Third Wheel?," 1.
17. Duke and Asher, *College Libraries and Student Culture*, 163.
18. Ibid.
19. Van Epps and Sapp Nelson, "One-Shot or Embedded?," 4.
20. Carlile, "Implications of Library Anxiety," 129.
21. Kolowich, "Missing from the Stacks."
22. Oxford College Library, "Research Instruction Classes."
23. Nunn and Ruane, "Marketing Gets Personal," 296.
24. Del Mar College Libraries, "Library Instruction."
25. Eugene McDermott Library, "Frequently Asked Questions."

BIBLIOGRAPHY

Armstrong, Annie. "Marketing the Library's Instructional Services to Teaching Faculty: Learning from Teaching Faculty Interviews." In *College Libraries and Student Culture: What We Now Know,* edited by Lynda M. Duke and Andrew D. Asher, 31–48. Chicago, IL: American Library Association, 2011.

Asher, Andrew, Susan Miller, Mariana Regalado, and Maura A. Smale. "Feeling Like a Third Wheel? Leveraging Faculty–Student–Librarian Relationships for Student Success." Poster presented at the Association of College and Research Libraries 2011 National Conference, Philadelphia, March 30–April 2, 2011. www.erialproject.org/wp-content/uploads/2011/04/ACRL2011poster .pdf.

Association of College and Research Libraries. "Information Literacy Competency Standards for Higher Education." American Library Association. Last updated January 18, 2000. www.ala.org/acrl/standards/informationliteracycompetency.

Carlile, Heather. "The Implications of Library Anxiety for Academic Reference Services: A Review of the Literature." *Australian Academic and Research Libraries* 38, no. 2 (2007): 129–147.

Cooke, Nicole A. "Becoming an Andragogical Librarian: Using Library Instruction as a Tool to Combat Library Anxiety and Empower Adult Learners." *New Review of Academic Librarianship* 16, no. 2 (2010): 208–227.

———. "Professional Development 2.0 for Librarians: Developing an Online Personal Learning Network (PLN)." World Library and Information Congress: 77th IFLA General Conference and Assembly. Submitted May 31, 2011. http://conference .ifla.org/past/ifla77/200-cooke-en.pdf.

Del Mar College Libraries. "Library Instruction." Del Mar College. Last updated February 27, 2014. http://library.delmar.edu/library/libInstruction.html.

Department of Information and Communications. "LearnHigher CETL: Information Literacy." Manchester Metropolitan University. 2007. www.learnhigher.mmu .ac.uk/research/InfoLit-Literature-Review.pdf.

Duke, Lynda M., and Andrew D. Asher. *College Libraries and Student Culture: What We Now Know.* Chicago, IL: American Library Association, 2011.

Eugene McDermott Library. "Frequently Asked Questions about Library Instruction." University of Texas–Dallas. Accessed May 7, 2014. www.utdallas.edu/library/ services/instruction_faq.html.

Francis, Mary. "Fulfillment of a Higher Order." *College and Research Libraries News* 71, no. 3 (2010): 140–159.

Gilton, Donna L. "Information Literacy Instruction: A History in Context." University of Rhode Island. Accessed May 1, 2014. www.uri.edu/artsci/lsc/Faculty/gilton/ InformationLiteracyInstruction-AHistoryinContext.htm.

Hovious, Amanda. "The Key to Information Literacy? Help-Seeking." *Designer Librarian* (blog), March 22, 2013. http://designerlibrarian.wordpress.com/2013/03/22/the-key-to-information-literacy-help-seeking.

Kappus, Theresa, Kelly Jenks, and Adrian Pauw. "'Can You Meet with Me on Friday?' Personalized Library Instruction by Appointment." *Alki* 27, no. 3 (2011): 8.

Kolowich, Steve. "Missing from the Stacks." *Inside Higher Ed*, April 1, 2011. www.insidehighered.com/news/2011/04/01/hispanic_college_students_and_university_libraries#ixzz2VHZTA17a.

Mellon, Constance A. "Library Anxiety: A Grounded Theory and Its Development." *College and Research Libraries* 47, no. 2 (1986): 160–165.

Miller, Susan, and Nancy Murillo. "Why Don't Students Ask Librarians for Help? Undergraduate Help-Seeking Behavior in Three Academic Libraries." In *College Libraries and Student Culture: What We Now Know*, edited by Lynda M. Duke and Andrew D. Ashe, 49–70. Chicago, IL: American Library Association, 2011.

Miller, William. "Introduction: Serving Underserved Populations." *Reference Librarian* 50, no. 1 (2009): 1–3. doi:10.1080/02763870802546332.

Nunn, Brent, and Elizabeth Ruane. "Marketing Gets Personal: Promoting Reference Staff to Reach Users." *Journal of Library Administration* 51, no. 3 (2011): 291–300.

Oxford College Library. "Research Instruction Classes." Emory Libraries and Information Technology. Accessed June 13, 2014. http://oxford.library.emory.edu/research-learning/instruction-classes/index.html.

Shumaker, David, and Mary Talley. "Models of Embedded Librarianship Final Report." Special Libraries Association. June 30, 2009. www.sla.org/pdfs/EmbeddedLibrarianshipFinalRptRev.pdf.

Stephens, Jason. "Why Students Plagiarize" [video webcast]. Turnitin. 2013. http://pages.turnitin.com/Plagiarism_45_archive.html.

Van Epps, Amy, and Megan Sapp Nelson. "One-Shot or Embedded? Assessing Different Delivery Timing for Information Resources Relevant to Assignments." *Evidence Based Library and Information Practice* 8, no. 1 (2013): 4–18. http://ejournals.library.ualberta.ca/index.php/EBLIP/article/view/18027.

Woodworth, Andy. "Why Your Library Should Do One-on-One Appointments." *Agnostic, Maybe* (blog), August 10, 2011. http://agnosticmaybe.wordpress.com/2011/08/10/why-your-library-should-do-one-on-one-appointments.

VALERIE FREEMAN

4
Embedded Librarianship and the Personal Librarian

"CHANGE PUSHES ACADEMIC LIBRARIANSHIP ONWARD," AND with the dramatic technological changes over the previous few decades, change became an imperative.[1] The idea of embedded librarianship began to gain steam in the late 1990s. One of the early "call to arms" came from Donald Beagle in 2000, in "Web-Based Learning Environments: Do Libraries Matter?" At that time, the World Wide Web was a new and barely tapped resource, though its "potential as an instructional tool and learning environment has attracted intense academic interest and commercial development."[2] Noting a convergence of important factors—a growing pressure for institutions of higher education to expand their distance education, initiatives that also attracted on-campus students—Beagle provides an overview of the state of online learning in the late 1990s. He concludes that while the increase in online learning also increases expectations for library support, there coexists an "assumption of minimal library involvement and access."[3] A minor finding of his, however, is a small but strong voice in the library literature that advocates thinking outside the box in order to take a broader approach to providing library services to accommodate web-based learning and maintains that "libraries [can] play an active interpretive or facilitative role."[4]

The dramatic increase in the number of students enrolled in online learning endeavors makes it imperative for librarians to change their method of reaching students. According to a Sloan Consortium report in 2003, 1.6 million students took at least one class online in the fall of 2002. This number represents just 11 percent of the total students taking classes that semester.[5] In fall 2006, according to York and Vance, 3.5 million American college students, or 20 percent of college students, were enrolled in online classes. This represents a 10 percent increase over the previous year.[6] By the fall term of 2009, the number of students taking at least one class online had increased to 5.6 million, representing almost 30 percent of the students enrolled in classes at that time. This is an increase of 1 million students over the term one year before. In another very telling statistic, this is a 21 percent increase over a single year compared with a 2 percent increase in students enrolled in higher education.[7] The more recent numbers, for 2012, show a potentially slowing rate of increase of 9.3 percent over the year before. The rate of students taking at least one online course is at an all-time high, at 32 percent, or 6.7 million.[8] As more students access their classrooms off campus, and despite easy access by most libraries to online collections, "students are *45 times* [emphasis added] more likely to start information searches on Web search engines than on the library Web site" and are more likely to learn about new sources from a friend than from a library website.[9] These statistics themselves present a stark image, clearly illuminating a need for librarians to take their services out of the library and to the user.

David Shumaker adds a layer of urgency to the already time-sensitive circumstances when he expands on the idea that librarianship is changing and that librarians of all stripes need to change in similar ways.[10] One of these changes, he argues, is creating a "path" to providing "value" by partnering "with groups of information users."[11] Increased online classes mean fewer reasons to go to the physical library. Indeed, twice as many students get information from friends instead of library resources.[12] The need for change goes beyond institutions of higher education. Shumaker argues compellingly that there exists a disconnect in the profession, that librarians and information professionals do not communicate enough with each other. Many libraries and organizations in which librarians work are not represented by the general classifiers of public or academic. These especially include organizations in the private sector; the work that medical librarians have done, for example, is frequently not included in the library literature but rather in the medical journals. Clearly, in this situation, dramatic change needs to happen; in Shumaker's words, all sectors of the library profession need to "travel, together, in the same direction."[13]

For her part, Lynn Marie Rudasill argues for a broad definition of embedded librarianship, that the term *embeddedness* carries with it certain implications of "sharing in the life of the department or program, understanding the dynamics of relationships between departments or departments and higher administrators."[14] Included in her definition are the frequently unmeasured activities of workshop participation, committee membership, conference representation, and others. Rudasill argues that these activities, though not addressed as such by the Association of Research Libraries, are critical to "the organization and dissemination of information that is the essence of librarianship."[15] In short, Rudasill's definition of *embeddedness* covers more characteristics of librarianship than do many others.

Writing in 2010, Drewes and Hoffman highlight that "embedded librarianship" had become a "prominent buzz word" in the previous five years, making its way into articles, conference presentations, and online discussions. Important to note are that the literature on embedded librarianship represents a wide variety of actions and approaches and that the very definition of the term, much less the goals and methods of its practitioners, is difficult to pin down.[16] Any exploration of embedded librarianship needs to attempt a definition, though.

WHAT IS EMBEDDED LIBRARIANSHIP?

In 2013, Stephanie Ball wrote an article titled "What Do War and Embedded Librarianship Have in Common?" in which she drew direct connections between embedded journalists and embedded librarians. A lieutenant colonel who was asked about embedded journalists in 2004 cited a need to dominate the "information environment" as a strategic move in warfare, and the embedded journalists aided in that effort.[17] The term *embedded journalist* refers to a reporter being "attached to a military unit in armed conflict."[18] Even more, such journalists are "metaphorically in the trenches" with those doing the actual fighting, all with the goal of creating a healthy and reliable "information environment."[19]

In short, *embedded librarian* came to be the term used for "deeply integrated librarian" in 2004 by Barbara Dewey.[20] It is also she who made the direct correlation between the intense collaboration between librarians and faculty and that of journalists with units in the Iraq War.[21] In the realm of law libraries, Ball considers the potential role of embedded librarians—that by understanding the goals of their surrounding groups, "librarians can be the machine that fuels the knowledge engine."[22] Shumaker cites Jezmynne Dene's definition of an embedded librarian as "an integral part to the whole."[23] While somewhat general in one sense, this definition does encapsulate the essence of the practice of embedding librarians into programs, classes, and departments.

So what does it mean for a librarian to be embedded? As embedded journalists enter a "reporting environment," often accompanying military units into war zones, so too do embedded librarians enter the "user environment" in order to best provide services to their clients at the point of need and maintain a user-centric approach to library resources and services.[24] In their article "Creating Opportunities: Embedded Librarians," Martin A. Kesselman and Sarah Barbara Watstein go into some detail to explore these definitions. Reflecting the wide variety of efforts and circumstances behind embedding, their definition of "the embedded librarian" is suitably complex. With a nod at the ideological connection to embedded journalists, wherein the "embedded librarian provides better access for students to him/herself and to the library's resources,"[25] David Shumaker provided a general definition to participants in a study that, regardless of title, if a librarian regularly participates in, and provides information services for, a community of mostly nonlibrarians, then the librarian is participating in embedded librarianship.[26]

There are a couple of models of embedded librarianship. The traditional model is the embedded program intended to bridge the gap "between libraries and distance learners, teaching faculty, and lab researchers."[27] This model takes advantage of the increasing number of web-based learning environments and fills a service need as colleges and universities dramatically increase their distance education options. Frequently, though not always, embedded librarianship amounts to an extension of the duties of subject specialists. According to Lynn Marie Rudasill, there exists a drive to embed librarians in their subject departments, resulting in "changing . . . the way subject librarianship is being provided to the users."[28] In the case studies she examined, the subject specialists still fulfill preexisting duties such as maintaining reference hours and delivering instruction sessions, but now also have duties outside the library, embedded in a department or program, allowing a more personal level of interaction between the librarian and faculty and staff of that department.[29] Within these general models, there is also plenty of room for creativity in program development.

There is a spectrum of levels of embedding, from the "macro-" to "micro-" levels. The macro-level is the one probably most frequently associated with embeddedness. This level is largely digital, usually involves a subject guide, and embeds the librarian into the online class management system. The process is work-intensive on the front end but requires little in the way of maintenance for the librarian. At the other end of the spectrum is embedding at the micro-level. This level allows more interaction between student and librarian, also usually in an online capacity. Collaboration between librarian and faculty is vital for this approach to work, especially to allow the librarian to provide a more tailored set of services to the students. It does also, however, occupy a great deal of the librarian's time.[30]

There is a belief among most librarians that targeted and contextual instruction provides better results than the general one-shot sessions. Embedded librarianship provides an opportunity to accommodate that need.[31] Indeed, our argument here is that a personal librarian program does what embedded librarianship does in this regard and much more. The individual elements of embedded librarianship include "teamwork, content knowledge, accessibility, adaptability, and responsiveness" but can look very different in implementation.[32] While many factors come into play with embedded librarianship (e.g., who provides performance reviews, where services are provided), at its core, embedded librarians are "integrated into their settings."[33]

WHAT OTHER LIBRARIES ARE DOING

As discussed, there are countless approaches to creating a successful embedded program for a library. A brief excursion through some successful programs is in order now to provide some examples of the general models. Again, one needs to keep in mind the important role that embedded librarianship has played as a stepping stone for creating a personal librarian program. At the macro-end of the scale is the traditional program at Valdosta State University's Odum Library. In the online environment, a professor had seen a need for students to have the instruction that was provided to the in-class students but recognized the challenge in fulfilling that need. Because of an existing relationship, he reached out to a particular librarian. The resulting program had librarians embedded in the online module of classes, both distance and on campus, that had a research component.[34]

In a world of entrepreneurship and where each step forward counts, the University of Toronto and the MaRS Discovery District (a hub of entrepreneurial activity) teamed up to create a program to address a "need to accelerate Canada's performance in the global knowledge economy."[35] Supported by national and state governments, MaRS is an important component in Canada's effort to build a knowledge economy with social and economic prosperity. With the University of Toronto as a founding member and strong supporter, both institutions stand to gain. When MaRS approached the university library with a proposal that presented a change from the usual approach to librarianship, the library found that the extended services requested, to provide information services to MaRS clients, melded well with its mission, even if not explicitly mentioned. In this new venture, MaRS helped fund a librarian whose responsibilities would be split 80/20 with the university. In short, the librarian primarily works from the MaRS corporate office but as a librarian of the university also retains responsibilities there.[36] This arrangement demonstrates what some creativity and flexibility can accomplish and the effects it can have outside an institution of higher learning.

One interesting example of a flexible program that alters its approach as needed is that of the Multidisciplinary Action Program (MAP) at the University of Michigan. MAP is an "action-based learning program for full-time first-year MBA students."[37] Early in the program, the students are unfamiliar with the wealth of resources the library has to offer. At its outset, this program was an effort at instruction, training students on finding resources appropriate for their studies. Because of the size of the student body, it was deemed early on that the librarian initially tasked with handling the instruction services was not sufficient. The needs could also not be met with traditional reference services. Then came the idea that the librarian working with the students could create specific training tools for these students. It still fell to a single librarian, however, to handle all the teams of students in the program. Eventually, the director decided to have more librarians involved in the program, dividing the large number of teams among up to eight librarians.[38] This changing program altered to fit the needs of the students and faculty.

The embedded program at the University of Calgary looks largely like a highly successful liaison program as well and provides a glowing example of a successful pilot program that was so well received that dramatic expansion ensued. What began with the English Department grew to programs with five other departments in a short time. The services offered in each individual program differed "based on the needs and resources available."[39] Not a centrally run program, though supported by library administration, the subject specialists responsible were free to create the program they thought was best suited to each department and adapt to the needs as they saw fit. Resulting differences included the existence of office hours for some subject specialists, who spent at least two hours a week in the department with which they were connected. There was support for the office hours in some departments but not in others, with some concern that they might be "spoon-feeding" the students too much.[40] Those librarians who did not hold office hours but have had a successful program with their departments remained interconnected in both the social and educational lives of the faculty and staff they work with. By 2011, the subject specialists were being reorganized out of a central location and into program centers and no longer worked reference hours.

There can be no doubt that the new technologies that have come about in the past few decades have changed the landscape of librarianship. With so many online options, many tools are available to reach students and other patrons. Diane Cordell rightly points out the value of Skype (and, by extension, other videoconferencing tools) as just such a communication tool. With the video and audio both available, the tools allow closer, more personal interactions. Face-to-face communication is possible, even over the lines and wires that provide Internet connections. The tools can open up classrooms to additional guest speakers, enable more full communication between an expert and a researcher, and allow for greater depth of collaboration. They allow for connections of all kinds, spanning distances that before had been impossible.[41]

EMBEDDED LIBRARIANS AND STUDENTS

If the point of embedded programs, whatever structure they take, is to maximize effectiveness of librarian efforts while fulfilling the library goals of supporting education and research, an important factor in the equation is the connection between embedded librarians and the students they work with. Again, the parallel to a personal librarian program is fairly self-evident. It is critical to understand the place of students in this structure and what preconceived notions they bring to the table. Research shows that while students benefit from offerings by libraries and librarians, librarians are frequently not seen as essential mentors for research. One possible explanation for this disconnect is the respective approaches to research by these two populations; librarians prefer a thorough approach to research, while students place more value on efficiency.[42] The common refrain of students who come in at the last minute for just enough research to complete their assignment is common to all librarians and reflects this tendency.

The effect of any embedded program on the students it aims to assist is the point at which most embedded programs will either prove successful or not. Some of that impact can be determined by the point in a student's degree program where the instruction interaction is taken. A high point of need is early in a degree-seeking program.[43] Early in the process of learning to research, students frequently struggle with both big picture and basic information gathering issues, both of which are skills introduced and fostered by librarians.[44] Doing so early allows these skills to be more thoroughly integrated into students' academic and research habits over the course of their academic career, and hopefully beyond.

The benefits of embedding can be multifaceted and do depend on the style of the embedment. For one, meeting the student at the point of need, online or in the classroom, lessens the time needed for the reference interview, in theory, because the librarian already knows the assignment and context. The embedded librarian can also stand ahead of trouble spots and offer proactive assistance. One of the criticisms of this simple or basic level of embedding is the lack of personalized service and human contact. This can inhibit students from developing their own search skills sufficiently.[45] A curriculum-integrated approach, in contrast, potentially reaches more students than the collaborative approach.[46]

A successful embedded program can also impact the interactions at the reference desk, though how might depend on the structure of the program. Moving library service out of the library has been found to bring a closer relationship between users and librarians (increased reference traffic, use of electronic course reserves, and other services).[47] The further removed librarians are from the classroom, the less they know about specific assignments, which results in time spent by the student in explaining the assignment need. An embedded librarian, on the other hand, has a greater understanding of the assignments and can therefore provide more individual assistance. In addition, because of familiarity with the course, they can foresee potential trouble spots and create aids for them or otherwise get help to the students.[48] Having an embedded librarian does not necessarily result in fewer reference desk interactions and can even increase them (even if these may be virtual). One example of this phenomenon occurs at Capella University, an online university where, after implementation of a highly successful micro-embedded librarian program, the number of reference calls and e-mails dramatically increased. Though there is conflicting evidence in the research about how effective instruction and embedded programs affect reference interactions, there is some consensus on their effect with regard to the complexity of reference desk interactions. Many reference desk librarians are being asked questions with increased complexity compared to those in the pre-embedded days.[49] It is not clear whether there is causation here, however, as opposed to correlation between the developments.

Information literacy, addressed in greater detail in chapter 3, lies at the core of embedded programs. It bears repeating that there are several ways information literacy is addressed: traditional one-shot instruction sessions, instructional reference interactions, websites, tutorials and other technological approaches, and simple embedding in an online course management system. Beth E. Tumbleson and John J. Burke argue that the latter is the best approach. It offers the student a higher level of mentoring and guidance than does the traditional one-shot session.[50] Their argument stems in part from data that indicates students are more likely to turn to faculty for research assistance than to a librarian; faculty are seen as the "subject experts and set the assignment requirements."[51]

EMBEDDED LIBRARIANS AND PERSONAL LIBRARIANS

Embedded librarians and personal librarians can look very similar to the uninitiated. Both represent concerted efforts to address the rapidly changing landscape that is librarianship and higher education. Programs are often started in order to increase retention, better the student experience, and deepen the learning in a wide variety of classes. There are some important differences, however, largely in the focus and breadth of the programs. While they may overlap, usually at the micro-end of the embedding spectrum, they remain distinct ideas and approaches. It is perhaps worth briefly summarizing the similarities and differences in this regard.

First and foremost, many of the tools used in a successful embedding program can also be used in a successful personal librarian program. Practices such as close collaboration with faculty, embedding or linking in the online course management system, and spending time in the academic department are all useful tools for either type of program. Effective collaboration is a necessity for any vibrant library. With so many options vying for time, money, and space, it becomes critical for librarians to increase their visibility on a campus, whether physical or virtual. Ever-increasing accountability heightens the spotlight on the core purpose of education, to educate students. No two programs are exactly the same, in part because of the institutions involved.

The breadth of the programs is one main difference between these two approaches. In an embedded program, the time frame is generally one class for one term. The librarian provides guidance and assistance to the students through collaboration with the faculty. Yes, there are exceptions, such as the MaRS program previously explored, but on the whole the focus is on a fixed period of time, usually a couple of months. The idea behind embedded programs is frequently one with the librarian metaphorically in the trenches with the students, almost an idea of "I'm in this with you, and I understand the assignments so I can help you now." In contrast, personal librarian programs focus on building relationships with faculty and, especially, students, that will span their academic careers with the goal of getting students to turn to librarians for research, and other academic guidance, and to make personal connections with students that can begin to stand outside the classroom.

BEST PRACTICES IN EMBEDDED LIBRARIANSHIP

For the librarian it is important to keep in mind best practices when engaging in an embedded approach to providing services. Again, knowledge of these helps us as we think about adopting appropriate best practices to building the long-term relationships associated with a personal librarian program. In "Best Practices for Librarians Embedded in Online Courses," Starr Hoffman and Lilly Ramin provide a comprehensive list of specific practices, as do Amy C. York and Jason M. Vance in "Taking Library Instruction into the Online Classroom: Best Practices for Embedded Librarians." David Shumaker also provides extensive information in his book *The Embedded Librarian*. And, as we have seen earlier in the chapter, many schools are implementing some form of the embedded librarian. As many schools as are doing it, there are that many different sets of rules and policies, which leads to a challenge in coming up with a best practices list. Throughout them all, however, is a core set of practices that are the same across most programs. That list is as follows.

Lay the Groundwork

To have a successful embedding experience, it is critical to lay the groundwork for it. The first step is to establish that there is a need. Once a need is established, work on getting support for your program. This includes getting buy-in from library administration, as well as from the faculty you are targeting. It could, possibly should, include ensuring support from the department chair and other administration. Having such a support network in place when you start the program will greatly increase the likelihood of success. In addition, have a clear understanding for yourself, and other librarians participating in the embedded program, of what services you are offering. The most basic practice for embedding is doing so in the online portion of the class, through the course management system (be it Blackboard, Moodle, or any other).

Preparation

Once it is decided that you will be embedded in the online classroom, begin your preparations. Get the assignments so that you can proactively provide the assistance required. You might have to go outside your comfort zone to do this. With advance preparation you can chart the term and plan for potentially busy times. You also need to decide how often you will post or engage in online discussion. Weekly? Biweekly? As needed? It is recommended that, whatever your level of involvement, you start a thread on the discussion board specifically for library-related topics. And make sure your contact information is easily available to the students so that they can contact you directly.

Preparation also includes getting familiar with the technology you anticipate using, whether it is the online course management system, tutorial building software, or other software. Know what you will be using before the start of classes. Get training where you need it, both for familiarizing yourself with the technology as well as for building relationships with the staff whom you would turn to in case of a problem, such as the information technology services department.

Execution

As with everything in the workplace, good communication cannot be underestimated. The embedded librarian will usually be associated with a class online through the entire term. Communicate clearly with the faculty member, in advance, about what you will be doing. Ultimately, it is his or her class. For your program to succeed, his or her needs as well as yours must be met. Also, the more the professor believes in what you are doing, the more the students will buy into it as well. Take the time to introduce yourself early in the term so that you are familiar to the students and your accessibility is established.

Alongside good communication comes flexibility. The world of higher education is changing, with librarians and faculty both being asked to take on more duties, tasks, and responsibilities, stretching an already short workday even further. In this environment, it remains critical to be flexible to the needs of others and the unforeseen details that crop up, usually at the least convenient time. Be proactive. Anticipate issues as much as possible. Initiate communication; do not wait for others to reach out. Those who need assistance might be waiting for you to invite contact and might not even know they could benefit from a librarian's guidance.

To the degree possible, go beyond simply having a library tab or link in the online course management system, although this is a necessity. Having a tab makes it easy for students to get to the library page and thereby access library resources. One might also include resources on specific topics, direct interactions with students on a discussion board, collaborative assignments, and more. Truly interweaving your presence through the course will maximize the effectiveness of your endeavors.

Always remember, fear of the library is real, and it can exist even in the online environment. On the one hand, it might be easier for participants to ask for help online, where there is no verbal interaction required. On the other hand, digital text communication has limitations. Without the ability to read facial expressions, body language, and voice inflection, it becomes easy to misconstrue the meaning of an e-mail or posting. Take the time to make your online presence approachable.

Through it all, be aware of your limitations, especially those related to time. Budget cuts have introduced a new reality in many places, one of staffing and resource limitations. Where possible, though, recruit some help. Maximize your time management skills, spending time on high-value activities as much as possible.

THE EMBEDDED PERSONAL LIBRARIAN?

Though chapter 9 presents a more comprehensive list of best practices for personal librarians, some details specific to a personal librarian being embedded should be examined here. When embedded in a class, the personal librarian will follow the best practices described in the last section, as well as make efforts to personalize the service. This includes individual, personalized communication and follow-up. The personal librarian must also provide assistance that addresses and is sufficient for the students' needs. It is also imperative for the personal librarian to interact proactively with students.

As the embedded personal librarian works on the micro-end of the scale, a whole host of other in-person practices exist that become increasingly important. These include one-on-one meetings with students, an in-class presence, and sometimes increased collaboration with the professor on assignments and grading. In short, the personal librarian will engage in activities with the purpose of personalization, whether in person or online.

While this set of best practices is far from comprehensive it does strike at some key elements that weave through both embedded librarianship and personal librarianship. As we have seen, academic institutions have taken a general idea and tailored it to their own needs as well as their limitations. Funding and staffing are just two of the many hurdles to implementing a successful embedding program, but they are not impenetrable. With creativity and hard work, it is possible.

CONCLUSION

The lieutenant colonel cited earlier in the chapter noted that the military considered embedding journalists a bit of a gamble, even though the practice dated back a century or more. His superiors had considered his idea of reporters being given access to classified war planning sessions to be "sheer lunacy," but his efforts ultimately succeeded.[52] In the world of education, Peggy A. Pritchard argues that a discipline-specific approach to education is now understood to be "insufficient." Rather, development of information literacy as well as academic literacies (critical thinking, reading, writing, and application of information) needs to be built into curricula. However, faculty members are often ill-prepared, or unwilling, to support changes, often not realizing that there are those on campus who do.[53]

Any examination of embeddedness would be incomplete without a look at the potential pitfalls associated with the program. These range from concerns of librarian isolation from one another if they work out of their liaison departments to dangers of moving assets out of a central library and into individual departments. The first, argue Michael A. Matos, Nobue Matsuoka-Motley, and William Mayer, is a shortsighted fear because of "the extension of the library across the wider organization that brings richer rewards over time."[54] With the increased digital access to libraries, their holdings can be used twenty-four hours a day, even when the doors are actually closed. The researcher, however, can work from anywhere on campus or off, which means that the librarian must also leave the library in order to reach the patrons where they are. The practice of moving assets out of the library, specifically in the form of librarians holding office hours in their assigned departments, depends on a number of factors. If the relationship is already solid, with steady and strong communication emanating from the department to the librarian, the practice can gain traction. This does, however, require outreach on the part of the librarian to create the appropriate relationship. Additionally, with the expanded library service, coordination can be a challenge.[55] In some cases, it can reduce coverage in the library.

Before collections grew to a size where they had to be housed in their own structure, "libraries were located in academic departments."[56] Through a combination of factors, from budget constraints on collection development to technological innovations making their impact on information needs felt, modern academic libraries are further distanced from that model of department libraries.[57] The challenge remains, however, to provide resources and services when and where they are needed, whether virtually or in person. Embedded librarianship helps to close that gap between information professional and information users. A personal librarian program can take this one step further.

Online education is here to stay. Margaret Gorts Morabito provided a glimpse into the mind of educators and the public in 1997, when online education was perceived as almost a curious oddity. In reality, online distance education was established in the 1980s, growing naturally out of the centuries-old phenomenon of distance education.[58] Though distance education was originally print based, further technological developments in the 1960s aided rapid changes in it, until the birth of online education in both private and public institutions. In an effort to boost a fledgling technology, modems were often provided "with a free membership to one of the major commercial online networks."[59] At that time, e-mail provided a means of communication, an online education network called HomeLink provided online education for business training, and these were just two of the offerings in the realm of online learning.[60] By the 1990s, e-mail accounts were easily available and teleconferencing was becoming a norm, expanding beyond simple text to include sound and graphics.[61] Online education today is simply the latest manifestation in a long history of education, one that takes advantage of an onslaught of technological advances in recent decades. In this rapidly changing world, it is increasingly critical for institutions to be adaptable. This is true for businesses, museums, and law firms as well as public libraries, colleges, and universities. The practice of embedding librarians is one such effort to find a creative solution, one that might cause hesitation among its skeptics, but one that goes far in bridging the gap between library patron and librarian.

NOTES

1. Shank and Bell, "Blended Librarianship," 105.
2. Beagle, "Web-Based Learning Environments," 367.
3. Ibid., 376.
4. Ibid., 376–377.
5. Allen and Seaman, *Sizing the Opportunity*.
6. York and Vance, "Taking Library Instruction into the Online Classroom," 197.
7. Allen and Seaman, *Class Differences*.
8. Allen and Seaman, *Changing Course*.

9. York and Vance, "Taking Library Instruction into the Online Classroom," 197–198.
10. Shumaker, *Embedded Librarian*, xv.
11. Ibid., xiii.
12. York and Vance, "Taking Library Instruction into the Online Classroom," 197.
13. Shumaker, *Embedded Librarian*, xv.
14. Rudasill, "Beyond Subject Specialization," 84.
15. Ibid.
16. Drewes and Hoffman, "Academic Embedded Librarianship," 75.
17. Ball, "What Do War and Embedded Librarianship Have in Common?"
18. Ibid.
19. Ibid.
20. Wright and Williams, "History of the Embedded Librarian Program," 73.
21. Ibid.
22. Ball, "What Do War and Embedded Librarianship Have in Common?"
23. Shumaker, *Embedded Librarian*, 25.
24. Bennett and Simning, "Embedded Librarians and Reference Traffic," 444.
25. Kesselman and Watstein, "Creating Opportunities," 386.
26. Ibid.
27. Berdish and Seeman, "Reference-Intensive Embedded Librarian Program," 209.
28. Rudasill, "Beyond Subject Specialization," 84.
29. Ibid.
30. Wright and Williams, "History of the Embedded Librarian Program," 73.
31. Ibid.
32. Cordell, "Skype and the Embedded Librarian," 8.
33. Kesselman and Watstein, "Creating Opportunities," 387.
34. Wright and Williams, "History of the Embedded Librarian Program," 73–74.
35. Fitzgerald, Anderson, and Kula, "Embedded Librarians Promote an Innovation Agenda," 188–189.
36. Ibid., 190–191.
37. Berdish and Seeman, "Reference-Intensive Embedded Librarian Program," 209.
38. Ibid., 214–215.
39. Clyde and Lee, "Embedded Reference to Embedded Librarianship," 393–394.
40. Ibid., 396.
41. Cordell, "Skype and the Embedded Librarian," 9.
42. Tumbleson and Burke, "Embedded Librarianship Is Job One," 227.
43. Bennett and Simning, "Embedded Librarians and Reference Traffic," 444.
44. Tumbleson and Burke, "Embedded Librarianship Is Job One," 227.
45. Bennett and Simning, "Embedded Librarians and Reference Traffic," 446.
46. Ibid., 444.

47. Clyde and Lee, "Embedded Reference to Embedded Librarianship," 392.
48. Bennett and Simning, "Embedded Librarians and Reference Traffic," 444.
49. Ibid., 447.
50. Tumbleson and Burke, "Embedded Librarianship Is Job One," 225–227.
51. Ibid., 226.
52. Ball, "What Do War and Embedded Librarianship Have in Common?"
53. Pritchard, "Embedded Science Librarian," 373–374.
54. Matos, Matsuoka-Motley, and Mayer, "Embedded Librarian Online or Face-to-Face," 131.
55. Ibid., 132.
56. Jacobs, "Embedded Librarianship," 4.
57. Ibid.
58. Morabito, *Online Distance Education*, 24.
59. Ibid., 30.
60. Ibid., 30–31.
61. Ibid., 35.

BIBLIOGRAPHY

Allen, I. Elaine, and Jeff Seaman. *Changing Course: Ten Years of Tracking Online Education in the United States*. The Sloan Consortium. January 2013. www.onlinelearningsurvey.com/reports/changingcourse.pdf.

———. *Class Differences: Online Education in the United States, 2010*. The Sloan Consortium. November 2010. http://sloanconsortium.org/publications/survey/class_differences.

——— *Sizing the Opportunity: The Quality and Extent of Online Education in the United States, 2002 and 2003*. The Sloan Consortium. September 2003. http://sloanconsortium.org/publications/survey/sizing_the_opportunity2003.

Ball, Stephanie. "What Do War and Embedded Librarianship Have in Common?" American Association of Law Libraries. Accessed May 8, 2014. www.aallnet.org/main-menu/Publications/spectrum/Spectrum-Online/war-and-embedded-librarianship.html.

Beagle, Donald. "Web-Based Learning Environments: Do Libraries Matter?" *College and Research Libraries* 61, no. 4 (2000): 367–378.

Bennett, Erika, and Jennie Simning. "Embedded Librarians and Reference Traffic: A Quantitative Analysis." *Jounal of Library Administration* 50, no. 5/6 (2010): 443–457.

Berdish, Laura, and Corey Seeman. "A Reference-Intensive Embedded Librarian Program: Kresge Business Administration Library's Program to Support Action-Based Learning at the Ross School of Business." *Public Services Quarterly* 6, no. 2/3 (2010): 208–224.

Clyde, Jerremie, and Jennifer Lee. "Embedded Reference to Embedded Librarianship: 6 Years at the University of Calgary." *Journal of Library Administration* 55, no. 4 (2011): 289–402.

Cordell, Diane. "Skype and the Embedded Librarian." *Library Technology Reports* (2012): 8–11.

Dale, Jenny, and Lynda Kellam. "The Incredible Embeddable Librarian." *Library Media Connection* (2012): 30–31, 51.

Drewes, Kathy, and Nadine Hoffman. "Academic Embedded Librarianship: An Introduction." *Public Services Quarterly* 6, no. 2/3 (2010): 75–82.

Fitzgerald, Kathryn, Laura Anderson, and Helen Kula. "Embedded Librarians Promote an Innovation Agenda: University of Toronto Libraries and the MaRS Discovery Distrct." *Journal of Business and Finance Librarianship* 15, no. 3/4 (2010): 188–196.

Hoffman, Starr, and Lilly Ramin. "Best Practices for Librarians Embedded in Online Courses." *Public Services Quarterly* (2010): 292–305.

Jacobs, Warren N. "Embedded Librarianship Is a Winning Proposition." *Education Libraries* 33, no. 2 (2010): 3–10.

Kesselman, Martin A., and Sarah Barbara Watstein. "Creating Opportunities: Embedded Librarians." *Journal of Library Administration* 49, no. 4 (2009): 383–400.

Matos, Michael A., Nobue Matsuoka-Motley, and William Mayer. "The Embedded Librarian Online or Face-to-Face: American University's Experiences." *Public Services Quarterly* 6, no. 2/3 (2010): 130–139.

Morabito, Margaret Gorts. *Online Distance Education: Historical Perspective and Practical Application*. Metairie, LA: American Coastline University, 1997.

Olivares, Olivia. "The Sufficiently Embedded Librarian: Defining and Establishing Productive Librarian–Faculty Partnerships in Academic Libraries." *Public Services Quarterly* 6, no. 2/3 (2010): 140–149.

Pritchard, Peggy A. "The Embedded Science Librarian: Partner in Curriculum Design and Delivery." *Journal of Library Administration* 50, no. 4 (2010): 373–396.

Rudasill, Lynn Marie. "Beyond Subject Specialization: The Creation of Embedded Librarians." *Public Services Quarterly* 6, no. 2/3 (2010): 83–91.

Shank, John D., and Steven Bell. "Blended Librarianship: [Re]Envisioning the Role of Librarian as Educator in the Digital Information Age." *Reference and User Services Quarterly* 51 (2011): 105–110.

Shumaker, David. *The Embedded Librarian: Innovative Strategies for Taking Knowledge Where It's Needed*. Medford, NJ: Information Today, 2012.

Tumbleson, Beth E., and John J. Burke. "Embedded Librarianship Is Job One: Building on Instructional Synergies." *Public Services Quarterly* 6, no. 2/3 (2010): 225–236.

———. "When Life Hands You Lemons: Overcoming Obstacles to Expand Services in an Embedded Librarian Program." *Journal of Library Administration* (2010): 972–988.

Wright, Laura B., and Ginger H. Williams. "A History of the Embedded Librarian Program at Odum Library." *Georgia Library Quarterly* 48, no. 4 (2011): 7–11.

York, Amy C., and Jason M. Vance. "Taking Library Instruction into the Online Classroom: Best Practices for Embedded Librarians." *Journal of Library Administration* 49, no. 1/2 (2009): 197–209.

JO HENRY

5
Academic Library Liaisons as Personal Librarians

TODAY'S ACADEMIC LIBRARY LIAISON PROGRAMS ARE A MULTI-faceted mix of traditional librarianship blended with aspects of outreach, education, technology, and strategic support. The library liaison duties have evolved over the years to include features of embedded librarianship, information literacy instruction, electronic tutorial creation, library guide creation, and online course support, to name a few. Often the liaison is specialized in one or more subject areas. Contact with faculty and students is frequent and critical to the liaison's success. Because all of the activities are relationship driven, liaison librarians fit perfectly into the personal librarian concept.

While today's liaison has taken on diverse roles, the position's beginning was rather simple. The evolution of the modern liaison began in the first half of the twentieth century. While it existed in a few universities earlier, the concept began to take root as a subject bibliographer in the 1940s. It was in this decade, greatly due to World War II, that the concept of a librarian as a subject specialist expanded.[1] The U.S. State and Defense Departments needed detailed information on foreign countries and began to support academic libraries with specialized study of these places.[2] In addition to overseeing specific knowledge resources, these librarians were also involved in collection development and relationship building with faculty members to enhance their institutions' collections.[3] Thus, the library specialist, or subject bibliographer, became more prevalent.

The concept of a library specialist grew slowly, although by 1960 most major universities had some type of specialist on staff.[4] Throughout this growth, subject librarians were met with resistance from traditional or general librarians. However, a number of librarians were supportive, including Dr. Cecil K. Byrd (of Indiana University), who wrote the following in 1966:

> It is no longer possible to meet all the particularized needs of the university's faculty and graduate body without the aid of specialists. The appointment of subject librarians . . . would both insure more comprehensive book selection and upgrade and personalize services. Further, it would significantly enhance communications between librarian and academician, and between the library and academic centers.[5]

In 1974, Eldred Smith (then Director of Libraries at the State University of New York) wrote that there would be a growing number of subject specialists and that these librarians would "continue to increase the quality of academic library service."[6] In 1977, lifelong librarian and past American Library Association president Laurence Miller suggested library liaison work take place in a formal structure supporting a professor's "instructional needs."[7] The Reference and User Services Association (RUSA) finally gave credence to this type of librarianship by creating guidelines for liaison work in 1992.

Beginning in 2000, academic library liaisons would undergo widespread implementation at all levels of academia during the next decade. The liaison programs involved expanded technology usage, embedded librarianship, curriculum and accreditation support, evaluation methods, and information literacy instruction. While these duties continue to morph and expand today, the core of all liaison success is communication. Outreach or marketing is now an essential component of liaison work. Liaisons must seek out students and faculty in order to facilitate interaction. A personal librarian program enhances these kinds of interactions. Beyond simply communicating, the personal librarian approach propels the academic liaison toward a deeper and more meaningful relationship with constituents. This relationship furthers the liaison's ability to provide assistance and support. While not all personal librarians are library liaisons, liaisons are in a prime position to take over this role. Already in a setting that includes working with both faculty and students on a number of levels, all that liaisons need to do is make it "personal."

As a personal librarian, the liaison commits to a deeper relationship with users than is necessary when conducting one-shot information literacy classes, creating a library guide, or posting library resources on an online class webpage. While these tasks are a component of relationship building, the interaction is brief. Personal librarianship asks the liaison to develop a more meaningful, long-term relationship with students and faculty. This change affects all aspects of liaison work. These areas of impact include strategic support (accreditation, new course proposals, and administrative support), education facilitation, electronic support, subject specialization, collection development, and communication. Being a personal library liaison means developing a personal brand—an identity that is recognized by both faculty and students.

STRATEGIC SUPPORT

For academic library liaisons, strategic support is an area of increasing importance. It includes administrative support and involvement in new course proposals and accreditation. Libraries are increasingly required to help advance the overall operation of the institution in these areas. Liaison work in developing new courses ensures they include information literacy requirements. These requirements are all the more important as related to accreditation. Information literacy is a component of analysis for many accrediting bodies. Additionally, liaisons are called upon to provide accountability for resources to support a college or university through the accreditation process. Finally, liaisons and library directors must further the mission of the academic community by not only providing support but also validating their worth in support of academic success in the classroom. All these areas of strategic support are enhanced if a personal library liaison connects with a department and its faculty.

The accreditation requirements for colleges and universities stem from several accrediting bodies recognized by the federal government as well as numerous specialized ones that lend credibility to an academic institution.[8] The Southern Association of Colleges and Schools Commission on Colleges requires an institution to provide "facilities and learning/information resources that are appropriate to support its teaching, research, and service mission."[9] The Middles States Association of Colleges and Schools specifically mentions "collaboration between professional library staff and faculty in teaching and fostering information literacy skills."[10] The standards also mention incorporation of information literacy into the curriculum to facilitate students' "critical analysis and reasoning, technological competency, and information literacy."[11] This type of involvement means personal library liaisons must become deeply involved with faculty and administration to ensure accreditation standards are met. It is a process that begins with course creation and continues through implementation. It is wholly long term and requires personal relationship development.

One aspect important to administration is student achievement, and personal library liaisons can play a critical role in this area. Studies have shown that students are more confident and accurate in research after information literacy instruction.[12] While this success has been covered in greater detail earlier, it is worth reviewing here some of the research that supports it. In Rui Wang's study, 60 students who took an information literacy course showed a positive correlation in areas of scholarly resources, correct citations, paper grades, and course grades.[13] A larger study by Shun Han Rebekah Wong and Dianne Cmor in 2010 analyzed 8,701 students and found that student GPAs increased with respect to the number of information literacy classes they took.[14] The GPA ranged from 15 percent higher after attending one information literacy class to 50 percent higher after four classes.[15] Information literacy skills were directly linked to student achievement.

To teach information literacy, the personal library liaison must have access to students. To reach them, the liaison must establish a personal relationship with faculty members and administration. Once this is done, the likelihood of infiltration into the classroom increases. Likewise, the stronger the liaison relationship with administration, the better the chance of clearing a way for a credit information literacy course to be taught. Liaison success is a combination of relationship development and an understanding by instructors and administration that information literacy and research skills are a valuable component of student success.

Linked to student achievement is student retention—another key issue for academic institutions relying in part on tuition and other fees for operational expenses. Poor academic performance has been shown to be a primary reason for withdrawal.[16] The personal librarian can help in this area as well. For freshmen, having a personal librarian to assist with library basics, resources, and research needs adds to their chances of academic success. Studies dating back to the late 1960s have shown a correlation between higher grades and use of library services.[17] Retention is critical not only for undergraduates but for graduate students as well. Here too is evidence that long-term personal library liaison relationships with students make a difference, often to a greater degree than with undergraduates.[18] Graduate students' skills using library resources often get rusty if there is a gap since undergraduate work, and they struggle at the dissertation stage.[19] This is the point when many students give up the program. This failure is due to a lack of research skills, such as pre-reading literature to form a topic, not allowing enough time for a literature review, and having trouble choosing resources to support their ideas.[20] To help at this stage, librarians have used the "personalized research clinic" as well as group and one-to-one consultations for graduate students.[21] The implementation of a personal librarian is a perfect match for student retention at both undergraduate and graduate levels. In fact, this personal librarian relationship is critical to student success and achievement of institutional goals.

In sum, personal library liaisons have increasingly become involved in course creation, accreditation, student achievement, student retention, and strategic support of the institution. This is important because library cuts and justification of personnel and the library itself are often required. More than ever, developing relationships with faculty, staff, and students and connecting with others play a role in the academic librarian's duties. Without the effort to establish these bonds, the connection between the library and the core of the college or university may be lost.

EDUCATION FACILITATION

Liaisons are becoming increasingly involved in the educational role. They directly support both faculty and students by imparting information on the library, its resources, and information literacy issues. Liaisons are co-instructors in units within a class as well as teachers of one- to three-credit courses in library research skills. This role as educator can be greatly enhanced through personal relationships. Whether embedded in the classroom or department or involved in information literacy support and instruction, this personal, long-lasting relationship with faculty and students will have a positive impact on academic success.

One form of deep, personal involvement as a liaison is through embedment in a classroom. As mentioned earlier in this book, classroom embedment involves a liaison attending or co-teaching a class throughout a quarter or semester. Often librarians are classified as co-instructors or teaching assistants. Their duties may include providing information literacy instruction and research support, integrating information literacy into class assignments, and grading resource related assignments. Through the embedded experience, the liaison gets to know the students personally and establishes a relationship of trust and support. An example of this comes from Daniel Webster College, Nashua, New Hampshire, which decided to move beyond one-shot instruction and embed a librarian into a required English class. Initially, the librarian taught three instructional classes and took part in student conferences regarding grades.[22] The outcome was so positive that the project was expanded to teaching eight instructional sessions with the embedded librarian involved in pre-testing, post-testing, and grading of research papers.[23] As a result of the expanded embedment, only 2 percent of the citations used by the class were from unacceptable Internet resources.[24] This involvement of a personal library liaison markedly improved student performance, and the deeper the relationship, the greater the student learning. As made clear earlier and reiterated here, an embedded liaison can develop closer relationships with students to increase classroom achievement.

Liaisons can also be embedded in a department. Many have office hours during the week or even reside permanently in the various departments or colleges of a university to support the faculty in a more personal way. The significance of this personal relationship is documented in the experiences of a Murray State University Libraries business liaison. Anticipating an accreditation visit in 2006, in 2004 a full-time embedded librarian was placed in the College of Business.[25] Positive things happened over the next three years, such as inclusion in committee meetings, assistance with accreditation visits, involvement with new faculty tours, and course software embedment as well as invitations into classrooms for information literacy instruction and faculty professional development seminars.[26] In every way, the liaison status was based on a personal relationship that was deeply involved throughout the department's activities. After three years, the embedded experience ended (because the librarian was promoted), and all of the gains in penetration into the department and interaction with business faculty and students were lost. In one year after the withdrawal, total research requests from faculty dropped from 264 to 40, and student research assistance meetings dropped from 287 to 49.[27] It is clear that the effect of the embedment within the department made a significant, positive difference to both faculty and students and that these gains were virtually gone once the intimate relationship disappeared. This before-and-after example illustrates the importance of the personal relationship and how a liaison embedded in the department can make a significant difference. It also suggests the value of personal librarianship and its possibilities to connect and establish relationships with students.

A final aspect of liaison work involves teaching a credit course in information literacy. This once again moves beyond a few classroom visits to a longer lasting librarian–student relationship. With mounting evidence that longer lengths of library instruction positively impact learning and research skills, the one-course information literacy class is becoming another educational role of the liaison.[28] A credit course allows the personal library liaison to impart information on such areas as research topic selection, locating and selecting materials, evaluating resources, analyzing websites, creating citations, and using resources effectively. This moves well beyond a one-shot instructional class and enables the liaison to establish a long-term relationship with students. Positive results from credit information literacy classes have been documented. At Texas Tech University students improved 13 percent from pre- to post-classroom testing results.[29] At Hofstra University credit courses have also positively impacted student retention.[30] The success of course credit classes has led other institutions to expand their courses from one to three credits. Through the courses, liaisons have developed relationships with students and, because of this level of involvement, have contributed to their improved research, writing, and library skills.

The positive effects of the personal library liaison's involvement in classroom embedment, department embedment, and information literacy instruction are undeniable. No longer an addendum to learning, these librarians are taking on the educational role. The growth and depth of the personal relationships among liaisons and faculty and students are a part of this expanding role and cannot be ignored. As a result, the improved skills resulting from librarian involvement have given the liaisons credibility and secured their continued role as library educators in the future.

ELECTRONIC SUPPORT

Another area of liaison work is electronic support. Liaisons are involved in online embedment, tutorial creation, library guides, chat and e-mail reference, and course management systems. Many students work from home instead of going physically into the library. The wide range of electronic resources has made this a new reality. John B. Nann writes the following in his article "Personal Librarians":

> A personal librarian program directly addresses factors that we identified as affecting the numbers of questions, namely students' lack of experience in libraries and being afraid to ask for help. It may also create a more direct personal relationship that may help in dealing with patrons not in the library.[31]

Nann addresses the fact that connecting with students is a challenge, and more so when they do not even enter the library. With remote users and classes increasingly offered online, it is challenging for liaisons to become personal librarians. Still, it is possible and just as important as face-to-face interactions to facilitate student success.

Liaisons embedded in online classes must reach out to students, especially to distance learners. Studies have shown students would like to access research information quickly in order to spend more time analyzing and using the information.[32] Posting library resources and links to library guides online is a basic step to providing what students need. However, a personal librarian must go further than that to establish a relationship. One way is to provide a library discussion board. There students can post questions for the liaison to respond to, and everyone in the class can benefit from these responses. Both the Community College of Vermont and Capella University have successfully implemented library discussion boards for online classes.[33] A library forum created at Marywood University sent out course postings as an e-mail, which eliminated the need for the librarian or students to log in to keep up-to-date on information discussed.[34] In fact, a study of the Marywood program indicated that the majority of students liked having a personal librarian and found the forum postings useful.[35] Using online forums such as this is an effective way of connecting with the remote student.

Personalization also comes through including the liaison's name, contact information, and office hours in all chat, e-mail, and library guides. A 2013 study of community college websites indicates the importance of contact information on webpages in building trust and satisfaction with users.[36] In addition to the contact information, a chat widget can often be embedded into library guide software. This creates a link that connects the students to their personal librarian for assistance when needed. Moniz, Eshleman, and Henry's *Fundamentals for the Academic Liaison* includes detailed information on use and personalization of library guides.[37] The use of names facilitates relationships, and its role is discussed in greater detail later in this chapter.

Images and sounds can also personalize connections with distance learners. At a basic level, a link to the librarian's webpage for additional information, such as office hours, a photograph, or even an introductory video of the librarian, can be placed on library webpages, course pages, or social media avenues. Moving beyond the basics, some liaisons use video conferencing as an online information literacy instruction tool. This goes a step further in personalization as the students actually see the librarian during their exchanges. The University of South Florida utilizes video conferencing by appointment to assist students with research.[38] Some librarians have uploaded recorded instructional information literacy videos to YouTube as a way to make the distance relationship more personal. Other instructional videos created for online students can contain a personal component if narrated by librarians. These are used in the embedded online personal librarian program at Chandler-Gilbert Community College.[39] Librarians and online students can also interact through screen capture software to which the librarian's voice giving instruction is added. At Webster University in St. Louis, the phone reference includes an online webinar link so that students can see in real time how the librarian finds resources online.[40] Providing resources is not enough for the personal librarian embedded online—interaction with students is necessary.

Personal library liaisons can do much in the area of electronic support to connect to students and support faculty instruction. Taking a step beyond simply posting resources or library facts to venture into the realm of online interaction connects the liaison personally to users. Discussion boards, video conferencing, webinars, screen captures, and using names and images throughout webpages, courseware, and social media will familiarize students with personal library liaisons. All of these electronic tools can be utilized to strengthen the personal library liaisons' impact online.

SUBJECT KNOWLEDGE
AND COLLECTION DEVELOPMENT

While the personal librarian approach influences some of the aspects of liaison work to a greater extent, both subject knowledge and collection development are affected too. As the relationship between the liaisons and the faculty and students deepens, the frequency and depth of inquiries increase. In turn, the liaisons delve further into their respective subject areas and are able to expand the library collection to better match user needs.

Liaisons' subject knowledge is enhanced by personal relationships with faculty members. Faculty members are experts in their respective fields and can provide essential information to liaisons. As detailed in *Fundamentals for the Academic Liaison*, liaisons deepen their relationship with faculty by attending a class, sitting in on formal lectures, collaborating on research, and having informal subject-related discussions.[41] Interactions with faculty can lead to opportunities for liaisons to infuse information literacy into class assignments, assist with library resource suggestions, teach information literacy classes, co-teach with faculty, and answer research questions online, among others, all of which deepen liaison–faculty relationships. In depth, subject-related exchanges will take place only after a personal relationship has been established.

Having an established, long-term relationship also improves the personal library liaison's connection to the information needs of faculty members. In turn, the development of the library collection is enhanced. Liaisons work at various levels of interaction—some embedded and some not—with faculty. Some liaisons actually reside in the department of the university rather than in the library for a more intimate communication opportunity. A "hybrid model" including reference, embedment, and a collection managing librarian has also evolved.[42] At the American University, the Music and Performing Arts librarian Nobue Matsuoka-Motley felt the "causal contact" of her embedded experiences was "extremely beneficial" for collection development and other collaborations.[43] Another example involved Indiana University of Pennsylvania's education librarian. There the liaison coordinated two children's literature festivals and a book program in conjunction with the students that used and enhanced the collection.[44] These examples show that the greater the personal library liaison's involvement, the better the librarian will be able to meet user needs through collection development.

The relationship built with faculty and their departments strengthens the personal library liaison's ability to improve the collection. It also improves the liaison's subject knowledge and, in turn, chances to assist students with *individual* research needs or information literacy–related skills. All of this, once again, depends on the personal relationship between the liaison and faculty. A personal connection enhances the role of the library in these two fundamental areas of liaison work.

COMMUNICATION

At the center of all liaison work is communication. Without good communication skills, all of the other actions of the liaison are diminished. It is through proactive communication that liaisons establish relationships with both faculty and students. Good communication is critical for liaisons to establish a relationship that will benefit the students' learning. As Lorri Mon and Lydia Eato Harris state in "The Death of the Anonymous Librarian":

> Among educators, traditional ways of communicating are no longer adequate for today's students. . . . [S]tudents now prefer contacts through e-mail, Facebook, text messaging, and instant messages. If this represents the fast-paced, highly visible and social world of many college students and educators, then librarians serving these particular users can expect to face the same powerful expectations. . . .[45]

Today's academic librarian must be open and accessible to students and faculty. Successful personal library liaisons must actively seek out their audience.

Personal library liaisons should begin communicating with students during their first year at college. At the University of Richmond, which established a personal librarian program in 2000, the students receive a welcome letter the second week of class introducing their personal librarian and explaining how the librarian can assist with class work.[46] Included in these letters are the personal librarian's business card and contact information.[47] At Johnson & Wales University North Miami campus library, a wiki for first-year students includes library information.[48] Texas Tech University Libraries posts videos on YouTube, the library website, and Facebook of personal librarians discussing some of their nonwork interests in order to connect with students.[49] All of these methods help to establish a more personal connection between students and their personal librarians.

Contact with faculty members is also critical. Establishing new relationships may begin with faculty orientations. These orientation meetings may also rekindle existing bonds with instructors returning from summer break. Personal library liaisons should further their faculty relationships by finding time for coffee or lunch during the academic year. Attending faculty lectures and staying abreast of writings also further the bond and may provide topics for conversations. Establishing a trusting relationship with faculty is important. Initially, the level of trust is based on a person's looks and, as the relationship advances, how a person acts.[50] However, in longer relationships, deep trust can be achieved at the level of shared thought perspectives.[51] This is possible to achieve by building personal relationships with faculty. In turn, the relationships lead to opportunities for the personal library liaisons to assist in the learning process. Throughout the school year liaisons are interacting with faculty to incorporate information literacy into class assignments and assist with instructional sessions. Often this leads to a liaison being invited into the classroom for multiple visits or to take a co-teaching role. All of these inter-actions improve the personal relationship between the liaisons and faculty members. Acceptance of liaisons into the teaching realm is important for the liaisons to be able to impact student learning.

Throughout all of the exchanges with students and faculty, the continued use of the personal library liaison's name is critical to maintaining positive communications. Providing a name and title in an introduction is an easy way to connect with someone new or with a remote user.[52] Recent studies show that the use of names in chat reference and e-mail has a positive impact on the student's comfort level after the communication.[53] Additional studies support the argument that the "personal" component of librarianship leads to "increased user satisfaction."[54] Personal library liaisons' names and contact information should be listed in prominent places, such as the library website, online course webpages, and library guides, so students can easily connect if needed. Use of names furthers the personal connections and enhances the communication exchanges.

Personal library liaisons can also establish communication by leaving the library and going to places faculty and students frequent. Some liaisons are embedded in a department of the university. In this case, their permanent office is in the midst of department activity, and personal relationships are formed from this proximity. The relationships formed by the business liaison embedded in the College of Business and Public Affairs at Murray State University led to increased requests for a variety of library services.[55] Liaisons can also be located in other buildings once or twice a week to increase rela-tions with departments. This was tried at Murray State University's College of Science, Engineering and Technology when in 2009 a new building was constructed with a library center.[56] It was staffed two half-days a week by a liaison, and her presence resulted in increased information literacy sessions and research assistance as well as improved faculty relations.[57] Roaming ref-erence is another outreach concept. Texas Tech created a reference cart on wheels that was sent out onto campus and guided by librarians with wirelessly connected laptops.[58] At Drexel University, a Library Learning Terrace was located near campus residence halls that offered virtual learning and collabo-rative spaces for librarians and students to gather.[59] All of these are examples of establishing a physical presence outside of the library in order to promote a more personal connection with users.

Face-to-face communication, even in the digital age, is still an important component of being a personal library liaison. Susan RoAne in her book *Face to Face* states that "the ability to interact and connect in person in real time is increasingly important . . . because being able to do so has become so rare."[60] To be effective in face-to-face communication, RoAne also notes the importance of active listening and eye contact in the exchanges.[61] Donna Dale Carnegie states that smiling is also important in personal communication as it "opens [the] door . . . [when] seeking influence for positive change."[62] For personal library liaisons to help, the student must allow them access, and a smile often initiates the exchange. Studies support the importance of face-to-face interactions and indicate face-to-face exchanges are actually the preferred method for some students seeking reference help.[63] At Mississippi State University Libraries, "person to person exchanges" with faculty and students were linked to an increase in research requests.[64] Promotion of research assistance was also improved by face-to-face marketing of the service during instructional and orientation sessions.[65] In fact, in Anthony Chow and Rebecca Croxton's 2010 study, face-to-face communication for reference assistance ranked first among preferred communication methods by students and staff and second by faculty.[66] All of these studies point to the continued importance of personal communication and human contact when establishing a relationship with users.

It is only through the establishment of a personal relationship that liaisons can increase their effectiveness when assisting faculty and students. Initiating the first communication and making the personal library liaison name and contact information readily available are musts. Seeking out faculty and students in areas outside of the library also plays a role. While much of communication today is electronic, the importance of actually meeting and personally assisting the users has not been lost. Whatever the personal library liaison approach, it must be done with personalization in mind.

PERSONAL BRAND

One final consideration of the personal library liaison is branding. In the world of business, the concept of selling a brand has long been a part of marketing and sales. According to Karen G. Schneider, the idea of branding dates back to 1937 and Napoleon Hill's *Think and Grow Rich*.[67] Dan Gall credits naming the concept of marketing a person's career as *personal branding* to Tom Peters in 1997 (Peters's work includes fourteen books on management and achieving excellence).[68] Peter Arnell, marketing strategist, describes branding as follows: "[The] ultimate act of branding is to take something—a product or service—and make everyone aware of it, and its purpose, or intent."[69] Personal branding is creating a personal image that comes to represent who a person is and what he or she does.

Writings about the librarian image date back to articles in the 1949 *American Libraries* magazine.[70] These early beginnings of branding for librarians are nearly as old as the roots of business branding itself. More recently, it was the topic for an ACRL New Members Discussion Group at an ALA Midwinter Conference in 2011. From these talks the ACRL developed several tips to consider when developing a personal brand. These include the following principles:

- Create a plan to develop the identity.
- Use a unique name or tagline.
- Connect all social outreach to one webpage or blog.
- Allot time for continual image maintenance.[71]

Steven Bell, ACRL president for 2012–2013, believes it is critical to put the "why" in branding creation.[72] This "why" is the librarian's core belief and what "drives your message," and it should be at the center of a personal brand.[73] Discovering what this driving core is may take time for new librarians, and it also may change over time.[74] For personal library liaisons, the image that defines the position and services delivered can be as simple as "the education liaison" or more interesting, such as "the liaison of learning." Each descriptive title points to the liaison's involvement in helping the education majors in some way and yet brands the librarian specifically. Before using a personal brand, make sure it does not conflict with the academic institution's image.[75] Finally, keep in mind that whatever brand is developed, the librarian must be able to deliver it well.[76] Knowledge about the subject area(s) assigned is a must for an academic liaison.

Once a brand is created, marketing comes next. For the liaison in the role of personal librarian, getting the brand out to faculty and students is essential. A variety of methods of communication of the brand are available through social networking, blogs, newsletter posts, library guides, and webpages. Each communication should note the personal librarian's brand or tagline. For the brand to be successful, Arnell says it must do the following:

1. "Generate news"
2. "Retain current audiences [and expand] appeal"
3. Translate globally
4. "Demonstrate superior differentiation"
5. "Revitalize brand image"
6. Be relevant
7. "Live up to the . . . promise"[77]

In the library world, the brand must be relevant and interesting to the students and faculty. If the brand is tied to a blog or news releases, the information

Branded Librarians

Brett Bonfield:	"In the Library with the Lead Pipe"
Kiyomi Deards:	"Library Adventures of Kiyomi"
Andromeda Yelton:	"Across Divided Networks"
Joe Hardenbrook:	"Mr. Library Dude"
Steve Cramer:	"Stevebizlib" in "This Liaison Life: Adventures of the Embedded Business Liaison"
Brian Matthews:	"The Ubiquitous Librarian"
Michelle Kraft:	"The Krafty Librarian"[78]

should be current and newsworthy. Having a unique brand makes an academic librarian more appealing. However, a catchy name or tagline is no good unless the librarian can back it up with good information and service.

The goal of marketing is to build a community—in this case faculty members and assigned students—following their personal librarian.[79] This involves building relationships. The concept of "relationship marketing" implies that the relationship does not end when the service is complete but should extend into the future when both customer (or patron) and the service provider (or librarian) will need each other again.[80] This is directly tied in with the personal librarian who can achieve building a long-term relationship through marketing. Part of this strategy involves branding. Librarians want repeat business!

Defining the role a liaison plays as personal librarian through a special name or tagline is the essence of personal branding. This involves creating, marketing, and maintaining the brand and its followers. Always behind the brand must be the foundation of knowledge so when followers (faculty and students) ask for assistance, their personal library liaison can meet their needs. Finding a unique persona and marketing that image is part of being a personal librarian. Just as it works in business, branding can work for the next personal library liaison as well!

CONCLUSION

Communication is at the core of all academic liaison activities. When the liaison is also a personal librarian, this communication is deepened and enhanced. Throughout liaison work in the areas of strategic support, educational facilitation, electronic support, subject specialization, and collection development, communicating with faculty and students is required. As personal library liaisons take on their role, they should develop a personal brand to "market" their services and use it to stay connected with faculty and students.

The relationships personal library liaisons develop with faculty and students extend beyond one or two encounters. They are intended to remain over the time of a student's enrollment or professor's stay with the academic center. Yet, personal librarianship is more than simply knowing someone for a long time. It involves interaction. Whether that interaction is in person, online, or through webcams, it means understanding individual needs and developing a relationship in which an individual sees his or her personal library liaison as someone who is always there to help him or her with library needs. As evidence grows that deeper personal library liaison relationships improve student performance and retention, why not make them personal?

NOTES

1. Hay, "Subject Specialist," 12.
2. Ibid.
3. Ibid.
4. Ibid., 13.
5. Byrd, "Subject Specialists," 191.
6. Hay, "Subject Specialist," 16.
7. Attebury and Holder, "New Liaison Librarians."
8. U.S. Department of Education, "Regional and National Institutional Accrediting Agencies."
9. *Principles of Accreditation*, 31.
10. Association of College and Research Libraries, "Accreditation."
11. Ibid.
12. Harris, "Case for Partnering," 604.
13. Wang, "Lasting Impact of Library Credit Course."
14. Wong and Cmor, "Measuring Association," 470.
15. Ibid., 472.
16. Mezick, "Return on Investment," 562.
17. Ibid.
18. Ibid., 564.
19. Harris, "Case for Partnering," 601.
20. Ibid., 602.
21. Lee, "Research Consultations," 171.
22. Hearn, "Embedding a Librarian," 220.
23. Ibid., 221–223.
24. Ibid., 224.
25. Bartnik et al., "We Will Be Assimilated," 151.

26. Ibid., 152.
27. Ibid., 153–154.
28. Harris, "Case for Partnering," 608.
29. Hufford, "What Are They Learning?," 147.
30. Burke, "Academic Libraries," 168.
31. Nann, "Personal Librarians," 22.
32. Jackson, "Integrating Information Literacy," 455.
33. Matthew and Schroeder, "Embedded Librarian Program"; Veal and Bennett, "Virtual Library Liaison," 163.
34. Ismail, "Getting Personal," 249.
35. Ibid., 253.
36. Pampaloni and Bird, "Building Relationships," 24.
37. Moniz, Eshleman, and Henry, *Fundamentals for the Academic Liaison*.
38. Montgomery, "Online Webinars!," 310.
39. Kadavy and Chuppa-Cornell, "Personal Touch," 68.
40. Montgomery, "Online Webinars!," 310.
41. Moniz, Eshleman, and Henry, *Fundamentals for the Academic Liaison*.
42. Matos, Matsuoka-Motley, and Mayer, "Embedded Librarian," 131.
43. Ibid., 134.
44. Heider, "Ten Tips," 117.
45. Mon and Eato Harris, "Death of the Anonymous Librarian," 355.
46. Dillon, "Personal Librarian Program," 11.
47. Ibid.
48. Covone and Lamm, "Just Be There," 201.
49. Henry, Vardeman, and Syma, "Reaching Out," 399–400.
50. Levin, Whitener, and Cross, "Perceived Trustworthiness."
51. Ibid.
52. RoAne, *Face to Face*, 19.
53. Mon and Eato Harris, "Death of the Anonymous Librarian," 358.
54. Ibid., 359.
55. Kesselman and Watstein, "Creating Opportunities," 390.
56. Bartnik et al., "We Will Be Assimilated," 157–158.
57. Ibid., 158.
58. Henry, Vardeman, and Syma, "Reaching Out," 403.
59. Kilzer, "Reference as Service," 296.
60. RoAne, *Face to Face*, xv.
61. Ibid., 12.
62. Carnegie, *How to Win Friends*, 59.
63. Kilzer, "Reference as Service," 293.
64. Nunn and Ruane, "Marketing Gets Personal," 572.
65. Ibid.
66. Chow and Croxton, "Information-Seeking Behavior," 255.

67. Schneider, "Personal Branding for Librarians."
68. Gall, "Librarian Like a Rock Star," 551.
69. Arnell, *Shift*, 32.
70. Schneider, "Personal Branding for Librarians."
71. ACRL New Members Discussion Group, "Tips," 1.
72. Bell, "The WHY of Your Brand."
73. Ibid.
74. Bohyun, "Afraid of Marketing?"
75. Yelton, "Personal Branding for New Librarians."
76. Schneider, "Personal Branding for Librarians."
77. Arnell, *Shift*, 126.
78. Yelton, "Personal Branding for New Librarians"; Hardenbrook, *This Library Dude*; Cramer, *This Liaison Life*; Matthews, *The Ubiquitous Librarian*; Kraft, *The Krafty Librarian*.
79. ACRL New Members Discussion Group, "Tips," 2.
80. Gall, "Librarian Like a Rock Star," 552.

BIBLIOGRAPHY

ACRL New Members Discussion Group. "Tips: Personal Branding and Digital Identities for New Librarians." Association of College and Research Libraries. Accessed May 24, 2013. http://connect.ala.org/files/66007/acrl_nmdg _alamw11_handout_pdf_68737.pdf.

Arnell, Peter. *Shift: How to Reinvent Your Business, Your Career, and Your Personal Brand.* New York: Broadway Books, 2010.

Association of College and Research Libraries. "Accreditation: Information Literacy and Accreditation Agencies." American Library Association. Last updated June 2011. www.ala.org/acrl/issues/infolit/standards/accred/ accreditation.

Attebury, Ramirose, and Sara Holder. "New Liaison Librarians: Factors Influencing Confidence Levels and Type of Activities Undertaken." *Electronic Journal of Academic and Special Libraries* 9, no. 3 (2008). http://southernlibrarianship.icaap .org/content/v09n03/attebury_r01.html#_edn1.

Bartnik, Linda, Katherine Farmer, Ashley Ireland, Lilia Murray, and Julie Robinson. "We Will Be Assimilated: Five Experiences in Embedded Librarianship." *Public Services Quarterly* 6, no. 2/3 (2010): 150–164.

Bell, Steven. "The WHY of Your Brand." *Library Journal*, January 20, 2011. www .libraryjournal.com/lj/communityacademiclibraries/888893-265/the_why_of _your_brand.html.esp.

Bohyun, "Afraid of Marketing? How about a Tagline?" *Library Hat* (blog), January 27, 2011. www.bohyunkim.net/blog/archives/date/2011/01.

Burke, Margaret. "Academic Libraries and the Credit Bearing Class: A Practical Approach." *Communications in Information Literacy* 5, no. 2 (2012): 156–173.

Byrd, Cecil K. "Subject Specialists in a University Library." *College and Research Libraries* 27, no. 3 (May 1966): 191–193.

Carnegie, Donna Dale. *How to Win Friends and Influence People in the Digital Age.* New York: Simon and Schuster, 2011.

Chow, Anthony, and Rebecca Croxton. "Information-Seeking Behavior and Reference Medium Preferences: Differences between Faculty, Staff, and Students." *Reference and User Services Quarterly* 51, no. 3 (2012): 246–262.

Covone, Nicole, and Mia Lamm. "Just Be There: Campus, Classroom, Department . . . and Kitchen?" *Public Services Quarterly* 6, no. 2/3 (2010): 198–207.

Cramer, Steve. *This Liaison Life: Adventures of an Embedded Business Librarian* (blog). Accessed May 26, 2013. http://liaisonlife.wordpress.com.

Dillon, Cy. "The Personal Librarian Program at the University of Richmond: An Interview with Lucretia McCulley." *Virginia Libraries* 57, no. 3 (2011): 11–12.

Gall, Dan. "Librarian Like a Rock Star: Using Your Personal Brand to Promote Your Services and Reach Distant Users." *Journal of Library Administration* 52, no. 6/7 (2012): 549–558.

Hardenbrook, Joe. *This Library Dude* (blog). Accessed May 26, 2013. http://mrlibrarydude.wordpress.com/about.

Harris, Colleen. "The Case for Partnering Doctoral Students with Librarians: A Synthesis of the Literatures." *Library Review* 60, no. 7 (2011): 599–620.

Hay, Fred. "The Subject Specialist in the Academic Library: A Review Article." *The Journal of Academic Librarianship* 16, no. 1 (1990): 11–17.

Hearn, Michael. "Embedding a Librarian in the Classroom: An Intensive Information Literacy Model." *Reference Services Review* 33, no. 2 (2005): 219–227.

Heider, Kelly L. "Ten Tips for Implementing a Successful Embedded Librarian Program." *Public Services Quarterly* 6 (2010): 110–121.

Henry, Cynthia L., Kimberly K. Vardeman, and Carrye K. Syma. "Reaching Out: Connecting Students to Their Personal Librarian." *Reference Services Review* 40, no. 3 (2012): 396–407.

Hufford, Jon R. "What Are They Learning? Pre- and Post-Assessment Surveys for LIBR 1100, Introduction to Library Research." *College and Research Libraries* 71, no. 2 (2010): 139–158.

Ismail, Lizah. "Getting Personal: Reaching Out to Adult Learners through a Course Management System." *The Reference Librarian* 52, no. 3 (2011): 244–262.

Jackson, Pamela Alexandra. "Integrating Information Literacy into Blackboard: Building Campus Partnerships for Successful Student Learning." *The Journal of Academic Librarianship* 33, no. 4 (2007): 454–461.

Kadavy, Casey, and Kim Chuppa-Cornell. "A Personal Touch: Embedding Library Faculty into Online English 102." *Teaching English in the Two-Year College* 39, no. 1 (September 2011): 63–77.

Kesselman, Martin A., and Sarah B. Watstein. "Creating Opportunities: Embedded Librarians." *Journal of Library Administration* 49 (2009): 383–400.

Kilzer, Rebekah. "Reference as Service, Reference as Place: A View of Reference in the Academic Library." *The Reference Librarian* 52, no. 4 (2011): 291–299.

Kraft, Michelle. *The Krafty Librarian* (blog). Accessed May 26, 2013. http://kraftylibrarian.com.

Lee, Deborah. "Research Consultations: Enhancing Library Research." *The Reference Librarian* 41, no. 85: 169–180.

Levin, Daniel Z., Ellen M. Whitener, and Rob Cross. "Perceived Trustworthiness of Knowledge Sources: The Moderating Impact of Relationship Length." Paper presented at the Academy of Management Conference, New Orleans, LA, August 6–11, 2004.

Matos, Michael A., Nobue Matsuoka-Motley, and William Mayer. "The Embedded Librarian Online or Face-to-Face: American University's Experiences." *Public Services Quarterly* 6, no. 2/3 (2010): 130–139.

Matthew, Victoria, and Anne Schroeder. "The Embedded Librarian Program." *EDUCAUSE Review Online*, January 1, 2006. www.educause.edu/ero/article/embedded-librarian-program.

Matthews, Brian. *The Ubiquitous Librarian* (blog). Accessed May 26, 2013. http://theubiquitouslibrarian.typepad.com.

Mezick, Elizabeth M. "Return on Investment: Libraries and Student Retention." *The Journal of Academic Librarianship* 33, no. 5 (2007): 561–566.

Mon, Lorri, and Lydia Eato Harris. "The Death of the Anonymous Librarian." *The Reference Librarian* 52, no. 4 (2011): 352–364.

Moniz, Richard, Joe Eshleman, and Jo Henry. *Fundamentals for the Academic Liaison.* Chicago, IL: ALA Editions, 2014.

Montgomery, Susan E. "Online Webinars! Interactive Learning Where Our Users Are: The Future of Embedded Librarianship." *Public Services Quarterly* 6, no. 2/3 (2010): 306–311.

Nann, John B. "Personal Librarians: The Answer to Simple Patron Contact May Be Simpler Than We Think." *AALL Spectrum* 14, no. 8 (June 2010): 20–23.

Nunn, Brett, and Elizabeth Ruane. "Marketing Gets Personal: Promoting Reference Staff to Reach Users." *Journal of Library Administration* 52, no. 6 (2012): 571–580.

Pampaloni, Andrea, and Nora Bird. "Building Relationships through a Digital Branch Library: Finding the Community in Community College Library Web Sites." *Community College Journal of Research and Practice* (in press): citations from prepublication copy.

The Principles of Accreditation: Foundations for Quality Enhancement. Southern Association of Colleges and Schools Commission on Colleges. Revised 2011. www.sacscoc.org/pdf/2012PrinciplesOfAcreditation.pdf.

RoAne, Susan. *Face to Face.* New York: Simon and Schuster, 2008.

Schneider, Karen G. "Personal Branding for Librarians." *American Libraries,* November 6, 2012. http://americanlibrariesmagazine.org/features/11062012/personal -branding-librarians.

University of Arizona UA Libraries. "Social Sciences Team: Inside the Classroom." University of Arizona. Accessed May 12, 2013. http://intranet.library.arizona .edu/teams/sst/connect/inside.html.

U.S. Department of Education. "Regional and National Institutional Accrediting Agencies." ED.gov. Last modified May 5, 2014. www2.ed.gov/admins/finaid/ accred/accreditation_pg6.html.

Veal, Robin, and Erika Bennett. "The Virtual Library Liaison: A Case Study at an Online University." *Journal of Library Administration* 49, no. 1/2 (2009): 161–170.

Wang, Rui. "The Lasting Impact of a Library Credit Course." *portal: Libraries and the Academy* 6, no. 1 (2006): 79–92.

Wong, Shun Han Rebekah, and Dianne Cmor. "Measuring Association between Library Instruction and Graduation GPA." *College and Research Libraries* 72, no. 5 (2011): 464–473.

Yelton, Andromeda. "Personal Branding for New Librarians." *American Library Association New Members Round Table News* 40, no. 3 (2011). www.ala.org/nmrt/ news/footnotes/february2011/personal_branding_for_new_librarians_yelton.

JEAN MOATS AND RICHARD MONIZ

6
What Personal Librarians Can Learn from Other Businesses

IN THE 1980S, A POPULAR TELEVISION SHOW, *CHEERS,* USED THE theme song, "Where Everybody Knows Your Name."[1] The Cheers tavern, which wove its way into American culture, was popular with its patrons because they all knew one another. People like being recognized by either their name or at least by a nod. Why should it be any different in a library setting? What is it about a personal relationship that can add an extraspecial touch to our business dealings?

In 1973, Wachovia Bank & Trust of Winston Salem, North Carolina, was the first bank to start a personal banker program.[2] Dr. Thomas W. Thompson, in *United States Banker*, defines relationship banking or personal banking as focusing on turning indifferent, single-product banking customers into loyal multiproduct clients in an intense, competitive financial environment.[3] The bank identifies how best to serve the customer in as many ways as possible. A personal banker is assigned to each customer to take care of all retail banking transactions.[4] The point is that someone working at the bank knows the person who walks into the bank because of this relationship. That personal service touch is what makes people feel special.

Librarians can learn from personal or relationship bankers as they serve individuals, communities, and society as a whole. Being a part of a service profession means putting the customer or client or patron first. This psychological urge to help people find needed information has existed since the beginnings of the library profession. In some sense, all librarians are personal librarians to their patrons, especially when a connection develops between the two people. Librarians can be found in schools, public venues, and academic and special libraries. Each of these settings provides a point of service where in time a relationship can be formed, especially if the librarian reaches out to the patrons.

However, personal librarians in other settings can learn from the high service standards that their colleagues or those in other professions follow when fostering personal relationships with their patrons.

PERSONALIZATION IN THE FOR-PROFIT WORLD

The importance of high service standards and concurrent history of personalization with regard to the for-profit world is considerable and probably dates to the relationships made by the very first humans who traded goods and services with one another. Trust and knowledge of "the other" has undoubtedly led to many a mutual benefit. For the purposes of our discussion here, we explore how businesses and for-profit organizations personalize services in ways that might relate to and better inform our efforts to create a vibrant and meaningful personal librarian program or initiative. The coverage is not intended to be exhaustive but rather exploratory. We hope that these examples and ideas will spur further consideration of the topic and help awaken readers to the kinds of things that they might experience in other parts of their lives (e.g., when shopping) that might then be integrated into library services and a personal librarian program. We should also note that many of these ideas already overlap with initiatives that librarians have stood behind in the past. The purpose here is to raise these ideas to the forefront and make librarians more conscious of these efforts and how they fit into the kind of program this book espouses.

As noted by Banwari Mittal and Walfried Lassar in *Journal of Retailing*, personalization in the business context refers to "the social content of interaction between service employees and their customers."[5] Some librarians may be put off by the relegation of our roles as those between employees and customers, but the fact remains that in any academic library, the purpose of library staff being there is to assist students who are paying tuition. This is not to downplay our roles as educators, which have already been covered in depth in this book in relation to the personal librarian concept. Rather, we ask that even if you are skeptical, you still consider the possibility that these ideas taken from the for-profit world could be beneficial in fostering positive student–librarian interactions and relationships. The importance of social interactions and interpersonal relationships in the health of a given business and the chances that a customer, or in our case a patron, would return has been understood to some extent for at least half a century in the relevant business literature.[6] In more recent times, librarians have definitely begun to recognize the importance of this approach, and this is manifest in a wide variety of ways. For example, many institutions have added either cafés or "coffee areas" to their libraries. This is a direct response to the success that bookstores and coffee shops have had in making readers more comfortable. Ambience has become increasingly important in library design as a result of what has been learned.[7] Libraries have also gone to such lengths as to hire anthropologists to study user behavior so that services can be better tailored to student needs.[8] These are not examples of personalization per se, but they reflect a trend. In the not too distant past, librarians organized the library with the subconscious notion that it could be done "our way" and that students would simply have to adapt. This has changed dramatically, and the aforementioned examples serve to remind us that we have already shifted our focus away from collections to how those collections and services in general are utilized to meet *individual* patron needs. The change has coincided, as mentioned in detail in chapter 3, with our efforts to teach students information literacy skills and better integrate the teaching of these skills into our institutions' curriculums. Once again, a personal librarian program is just the next most logical step in this development.

When people in the business world speak of personalizing, they are not entirely, but more typically, referring to services as opposed to products. This is the emphasis here. One of the more promising and telling examples has been the effort in the for-profit sector to assess service quality from the individual customer's perspective. SERVQUAL, later adapted and renamed LibQUAL+ by the library community, is one fairly recent example in this regard. The original SERVQUAL instrument was designed to measure customer expectations against their actual perception of both how they viewed services and how they would like be able to view or rate services against five elements: tangibles, reliability, responsiveness, assurance, and empathy.[9] The LibQUAL+ version of this instrument, adapted for academic libraries, repeatedly used, and validated once again by a recent study by Miguel Morales and colleagues, seeks to consider users' affect of service (i.e., staff provide caring and courteous service), information control, and library as place.[10] In a nutshell, *individual* users and their perspectives matter.

Another of the recent efforts to build even further on some of the precedent set by both SERVQUAL and LibQUAL+ is the RQ, or relationship quality, scale. RQ measures the quality of a relationship through elements such as trust, reliability, and empathy (among other components). Furthermore, its creators usefully define *relationship quality* as "a measure of the extent to which consumers want to maintain relationships to their service providers."[11] Indeed, this is one of the goals that academic librarians seek through the creation of a personal librarian program—to create relationships that make students feel comfortable coming back for additional learning and information.

Perusing the marketing literature, one cannot help but be struck by just how significant the trend toward personalization has become and how quickly it is moving. According to Rosie Baker in *Marketing Week*, mass markets and the marketing of one-size-fits-all products and services are things of the past. In the future, we will see the continued development of personalization at a number of levels.[12] Eric Krell writes in *Baylor Business Review*, "Customers, more so than companies, determine the value of a product or service. Today, customers assign that value in large part on the degree to which they can customize and personalize those offerings."[13] For just one example, a recent examination of trends in the hotel industry indicated that "loyalty, cooperation, and participation from the customers are becoming more and more important elements in enabling service companies to build long-term relationships with customers."[14] Of course, many of these and other studies point to the influence of technology and the resultant raised level of expectation in terms of customer service. A decade ago the level of targeted advertisement seen through sites such as Amazon.com would have been almost unthinkable. Librarians have decried some of these developments in personalization as an invasion of privacy. The fact of the matter, however, is that younger students actually seem to expect and desire such elements in services. This is not to suggest, of course, that such services would be automated to the degree that the human is cut out. Rather, the rapid and ever-increasing success of such automated services cannot be denied. What is needed is a way to craft "old-fashioned" relationships while simultaneously connecting to students in a variety of ways as we prepare both them and ourselves for the future.

There is no doubt that librarians benefit from the myriad of electronic means by which they connect with their students. That said, there is a danger in the continued over-reliance on electronic services and the potential for either lack of personalization or the tendency to allow this personal component to be entirely automated. Many books, articles, and presentations have been written on the importance of face-to-face communication or, at minimum, communication that is truly personalized. One of the best short articles on the topic can be found in *American Salesman*. Alan Bayham highlights the importance of face-to-face communication and says it is better than other marketing techniques in that it allows, in his case and that of his readers, the salesperson to have the undivided attention of the customer and tailor the message to meet the needs of the specific customer, ensures that the message is at the level that a specific customer will understand, enables nonverbal communication, provides instant answers to customer questions, and manifests the ability to close with the customer directly.[15] This list could not be better for guiding a personal librarian program! Students are bombarded by messages in e-mail, through Facebook, on billboards, and so forth, so the relative value of *any* opportunity to have their attention face-to-face cannot be underestimated. By personalizing services a librarian can tailor discussion to the specific concerns of students relative to specific assignments or classes or, in the broadest sense, academic program and career goals. Standing before groups of students and sitting with them one-on-one creates a rich environment in terms of our ability to answer questions and take in nonverbal feedback. Finally, we have the chance to "close the deal" by ensuring that students walk away with something of value in the form of better sources, improved researching skills, and other goals that we have determined in advance. Furthermore, modeling professional communication can help to improve the dwindling interpersonal skills of our students as well. According to noted author Robert Hall, in speaking about the interpersonal skills of our younger students and citizens, "For the next generation of workers and customers, products of an electronic age, this emotional deficit will likely only increase."[16] Implied in Hall's statement is the idea that one significant by-product of having direct relationships with customers or students in our case is that we help them to develop their interpersonal skills. Thus, a personal librarian program has benefits that reach beyond simply making students comfortable with the library or able to find information. It makes them that much more adept at developing relationships themselves in whatever career path they choose.

"OUT OF THE BOX" EXAMPLES

Before concluding our very brief exploration of personalization in the for-profit sector, we want to share a few creative ideas that businesses have employed in the past. Some of these may be more easily replicable than others in the academic library environment, but all should be food for thought. Again, the intent here is to get you thinking outside the box!

One example comes from British Airways. In 2008, a time when most travel budgets were being tightened, the company's vice president, Anne Tedesco, was asked to promote more air travel. Somewhat congruent with our purposes here, the intent was to encourage more face-to-face interaction among customers, especially those clients who interacted with other clients overseas and could benefit from face-to-face communications. Anne created an event called "Networking in the Sky." The company gave away 900 tickets to a select group of 3,000 applicants.[17] It not only gave away the tickets but created a whole positive experience for these individuals that surely paid huge dividends in terms of word of mouth. Librarians cannot typically give away airline tickets, of course, but what could libraries do to create their own "networking in the sky" types of events or opportunities? Could this be incorporated into a personal librarian program?

Swipely, a company based in Providence, Rhode Island, focuses on assisting small businesses and is associated with the U.S. Small Business Administration. Swipely encourages people to regularly share business marketing ideas through its website and blog. One such idea, shared by Alayne White, owner of White Spas, highlights creative efforts to get customers in the door. White explains how she went to the local car dealership and the local burger place to surprise people with free gift certificates and information about spa services. Her focus in these encounters was not just to hand out certificates but also to meet people, talk to them, and both share what she has to offer and listen to their interests and concerns.[18] Once again, libraries do not have spas (at least not ours!), but what do we have? What could we do to go out and wow people while introducing them perhaps to their personal librarian or the personal librarian program? In what ways have we not considered potential small investments in time and money that could pay huge dividends to our students in raising their level of awareness?

One marketing idea shared by Lesley Hankin in *Money Marketing* is to regularly follow face-to-face interaction with short bursts of carefully tailored communication in another format, such as e-mail. For example, one might send a quick message noting what the rise in interest rates means or does not mean to a particular client's investments or how a particular bill that's been passed might affect their financial planning. Hankins's idea is not to overwhelm clients but to remind them that she is there to assist and to provide useful information in the process.[19] This is great grist for the mill in our thinking about a personal librarian program and how we want to reach out to students. Rather than just saying hello, what piece of information could we pass along that would be of critical use to that student? (Does it even need to be library related?) How can we add value and continue to maintain awareness?

Another promising example of how innovation and personalization can work well together comes from Michael Neill, president of Michael Neill and Associates Inc. in Atlanta, Georgia. Neill's firm has been engaged in transforming credit unions to be less focused on process and products and more focused on services, specifically personalized services. According to Neill, "When a member service representative says to a member 'I've found a way to save you money,' that's a lot different than saying 'Would you like to talk about a checking account?'" Furthermore, according to Neill, the "focus is not only on credit union profitability but on the financial success of a member."[20] In other words, while we are all focused on the well-being of our libraries, we really need to think very hard about the specific needs of our students. Likewise, a personal librarian program in itself is really just a means to an end. Instead of the credit union that focuses on clients' financial well-being, librarians would focus on the students' success in class and ultimately in life. The special focus should be, it might be argued, on their research and information literacy skills, but the broader success of the student must always be kept in mind as the bigger goal. The success of a personal librarian program and of the library then, in some sense, becomes the inevitable by-product of this focused attention.

One last example of personalization will suffice. As librarians we come across vendors of various library-related products on a regular basis (e.g., databases, supplies). These vendors need to bridge the gap between the business world and our libraries in order to be successful. As such, personalizing their services is of high importance. We have limited time in any given day. As such, we often resent cold calls from vendors who know little or nothing about us or our library's mission. Some companies have really taken this to heart and moved beyond such an approach. It has been my experience, for example, in interacting with EBSCO that *my* sales representative knows who I am, what programs my institution offers, what products we have purchased or used in the past, what other branches of my institution or similar institutions are using for databases, and so forth. EBSCO representatives are patient and always interested, and this is key in listening to what our library needs and challenges are. They then try to offer solutions or assistance any way they can. I am not sure what their training entails, but you get a sense that they want to help you. If they can sell more databases or services along the way, great, but that's almost a by-product. And it works! They do sell the databases. This is what we need to do with our students. We need to be there, like any good business, putting them first. The rest will come (in our case, use our resources and services to be more successful in their research). Too often in the past we have been equated to the "cold calling vendor" who knows nothing about us but is instead trying to sell a one-size-fits-all approach and/or product that may or may not suit our library's needs.

CONCLUSION

This chapter began with a discussion of personal bankers and ended with a discussion of credit unions and database vendors. It is by intent that it has run this gamut. The idea conveyed is to stretch out further beyond the walls of the academic library. Be creative. Do not think just about libraries but rather how much we might incorporate and learn beyond our traditional approaches and ways. Banks and other businesses, concerned about their bottom lines, have recognized the need to personalize services and have done so in amazingly creative ways. It is hoped that this chapter is just the beginning for the reader. Literature about special marketing and business in general should be something that librarians do not shy away from, especially those interested in developing a personal librarian program!

NOTES

1. "Cheers."
2. "Personalized Banking Gets Statewide Push."
3. Thompson, "Personal Bankers."
4. "Personalized Banking Gets Statewide Push."
5. Mittal and Lassar, "Role of Personalization," 96.
6. Ibid.
7. Woodward, *Creating the Customer-Driven Library*, 86–102.
8. Wu Somaly and Lanclos, "Re-imagining the Users' Experience."
9. Parasuraman, Berry, and Zeithaml, "Refinement and Reassessment of the SERVQUAL Scale," 423.
10. Morales et al., "Independent Assessment."
11. Roberts, Varki, and Brodie, "Measuring the Quality of Relationships in Consumer Services," 191.
12. Baker, "Personalization, Localisation, and Trust."
13. Krell, "Customer Service 3.0," 7.
14. Sahoo, "Integrating Customer Relationship Management," 58.
15. Bayham, "Six Reasons."
16. Hall, "Emotional Engagement," 7.
17. Daum, "Make It Memorable."
18. White, "Marketing a Spa."
19. Hankin, "Lasting Impression," 15.
20. "Deepen Member Relationships and Increase Profitability," 48.

BIBLIOGRAPHY

Baker, Rosie. "Personalization, Localisation, and Trust Are the Watchwords for This New Era." *Marketing Week* 35, no. 43 (2012): 7.

Bayham, Alan. "Six Reasons Why Face-to-Face Trumps Mass Marketing." *American Salesman* 53, no. 6 (2008): 22–25.

"Cheers." *Wikipedia*. Accessed July 17, 2013. https://en.wikipedia.org/wiki/Cheers.

Daum, Kevin. "Make It Memorable: Face-Face Connections Provide the Most Value." *Small Business Los Angeles* 6, no. 3 (2010): 8.

"Deepen Member Relationships and Increase Profitability." *Credit Union Management* 34, no. 11 (2011): 48.

Hall, Robert. "Emotional Engagement: Key to Customer Relationships." *ABA Bank Marketing* 44, no. 8 (2012): 6–7.

Hankin, Lesley. "A Lasting Impression." *Money Marketing* 68 (2007): 15.

Krell, Eric. "Customer Service 3.0." *Baylor Business Review* 30, no. 2 (2013): 2–10.

Mittal, Banwari, and Walfried Lassar. "The Role of Personalization in Service Encounters." *Journal of Retailing* 72, no. 1 (1996): 95–109.

Morales, Miguel, Riadh Ladhari, Javier Reynoso, Rosario Toro, and Cesar Sepulveda. "An Independent Assessment of the Unidimensionality, Reliability, Validity and Factor Structure of the LibQUAL+ Scale." *The Service Industries Journal* 32, no. 16 (2012): 2585–2605.

Parasuraman, A., Leonard L. Berry, and Valarie A. Zeithaml. "Refinement and Reassessment of the SERVQUAL Scale." *Journal of Retailing* 67, no. 4 (1991): 420–450.

"Personalized Banking Gets Statewide Push." *Banking* 66, no. 4 (1973): 16.

Roberts, Keith, Sajeev Varki, and Rod Brodie. "Measuring the Quality of Relationships in Consumer Services." *European Journal of Marketing* 37, no. 1/2 (2003): 169–196.

Sahoo, Debjani. "Integrating Customer Relationship Management in Hotel Operations—A Comparative Study." *Vilakshan: The XIMB Journal of Management* 8, no. 2 (2012): 57–70.

Thompson, Thomas W. "Personal Bankers: A Perspective." *United States Banker* (March 1984): 6–8.

White, Alayne. "Marketing a Spa: How Alayne White Gets Them in the Door." *Swipely Blog*, July 1, 2011. http://blog.swipely.com/marketing/marketing-a-spa-how-alayne-white-gets-them-in-the-door.

Woodward, Jeannette. *Creating the Customer-Driven Library: Building on the Bookstore Model*. Chicago, IL: American Library Association, 2005.

Wu Somaly, Kim, and Donna Lanclos. "Re-imagining the Users' Experience: An Ethnographic Approach to Web Usability and Space Design." *Reference Services Review* 39, no. 3 (2011): 369–389.

RICHARD MONIZ

7

What Personal Librarians Can Learn from Other Academic Services

ANYONE WORKING IN HIGHER EDUCATION RECOGNIZES THAT IT takes the efforts of an entire team of staff and faculty combined to create the kind of experience that our students need in order to be successful and make the most of their college experience. While the experience and knowledge provided by faculty, the quality of instruction, and the relationships with faculty are more typically paramount in determining the quality of a student's overall experience, staff and support services play a critical role. Sometimes this is more overt and sometimes more hidden. Librarians know that the degree to which students utilize services varies considerably. Some students may use the library every day for everything from finding books, sending e-mail messages, and checking Facebook to getting assistance from librarians in conducting research and writing papers. Other students come infrequently and only with perhaps a very quick or targeted need. One of the primary motivations behind the implementation of a personal librarian program is to increase familiarity with the breadth and depth of services and make students become more aware of the resources available to them. The reality is that many other departments outside the library are also doing creative things in this regard. That is, they are reaching out to *individual* students with personalized assistance relevant to their particular subject areas. Like we saw in the earlier exploration in this book of special libraries and businesses, these other departments have ideas and programs that could help library staff to think more creatively as they explore their own personal librarian initiatives. Departments and other institutional affiliates mentioned in the following discussion include academic support centers, information technology departments, career services, student financial services, and health services, as these areas seemed most relevant to our topic at hand. Again, the intent here is not to be exhaustive but rather to provide some flavor of the ways that personalization manifests itself elsewhere that could be suggestive of better ways to approach library-related programs, such as a personal librarian program, and/ or to integrate them into other successful programs on campus.

ACADEMIC SUPPORT CENTERS

Academic support centers have a long and rich tradition of helping students. Support staff share the ethos of service that librarians possess but have become adept at personalization by focusing more on relationships than on transactional encounters, as evidenced by the work they have historically done through tutoring, providing ongoing assistance for students with learning disabilities, and creating sponsored activities. Their services have long been provided based on an in-depth knowledge of student emotional needs and how students learn. According to Susan Komives and Dudley Woodard in *Student Services: A Handbook for the Profession*, famous psychologist and researcher Carl Rogers determined that certain types of relationships can lead to greater personal growth and change than others. Rogers states that "three personal characteristics or necessary conditions [are] of supreme importance: genuineness, or congruence; unconditional positive regard, or acceptance; and accurate empathic understanding."[1] Such understanding is fundamental to how academic support centers operate. This sounds very similar to our Reference and User Services Association standards, which emphasize active listening and having a genuine interest in assisting a given patron.[2] The standards form a good foundation as we move away from resources and transactional exchanges and toward a focus on building relationships on an individual level. By their very nature, academic support services tend to focus on offering opportunities for students to receive one-on-one attention with regard to tutoring. When interviewed by Joe Landsberger, Todd Philips, Director of the Learning Center and Title III Activity Director at East Central College in Missouri, said that academic support centers are charged with improving student retention and, ultimately, achieving success both in college and beyond.

He stated, "All want to create better students and teach transferable skills that they can take with them."[3] Among other creative strategies or initiatives attempted by academic support center staff, Philips was able to get the campus photo ID machine relocated to the center's space. While it may seem minor, this small tweak meant that *all* new students would have to come through and thus be at least minimally exposed to the location of and services offered by the academic support center. Philips went on to describe the importance of establishing strong, high-quality relationships across the campus for the benefit of students and taking a holistic view in forming partnerships with other areas. Specifically he stated, "I believe that learning centers add value to all departments, and all departments add value to our center."[4] This is a profound way to view services. A personal librarian program should seek to incorporate this mentality as well by both strengthening students' overall experience through their connection with the classroom and other school-related areas and by drawing strength from those areas in turn to seek improvement and integration of the library and its services.

While most schools have support programs for all students, it is interesting to note that many schools tailor some to specific students. For example, at-risk accounting students at Johnson & Wales University's Charlotte campus are most commonly targeted for special intervention, often with the intent of personalizing service to them and encouraging them to build a personal bond with someone on campus. This does not always have to be a regular full-time staff member. For example, students who fall into the at-risk category are often paired up with student tutors. These peer tutors establish strong relationships with the students through activities such as one-on-one tutoring. The university may even pay tutors to attend the class regularly so that they will be aware of the course content and what a given student's specific needs may be. Indeed, they are embedded in classes in the truest sense, following all that is occurring.[5]

A program reported by Aimee Mapes in *Journal of Adult and Adolescent Literacy* serves as yet another sample of what academic support centers are doing. A handful of particularly at-risk students at Mapes's institution were required to enroll in a mandatory program called the Freshmen Connection. The program targeted assistance with reading, writing, and research skills for approximately forty to forty-five students. According to Mapes, students from disadvantaged groups often struggle to build a confident identity in college. This is where the personalization plays a critical role. She states, "It is especially important to cultivate opportunities for students to draw on sites of authority in their lives within their formal education and to offer moments of agency in literacy."[6] Essentially, all faculty and staff, especially those in the library, need to get to know individual students and what makes them tick. By doing this and incorporating as much "active doing" on the students' part into a personal librarian program as possible, librarians can help students acknowledge their personal identity and build their self-confidence. It is thus not just the relationship with the personal librarian that is important in itself; it is also the positive relationship and sense of self that the personal librarian can assist in fostering that is key here.

One more example of how academic support centers target specific students should suffice. Some schools with prominent athletic programs spend millions of dollars a year providing personalized tutoring and assistance to college athletes. In fact, there are at least seventy-three schools in the United States that dedicate more than $1,000,000 per year toward these services on their campus. Some extreme examples are the $15,000,000 spent by the Cox Communications Academic Center for Student Athletes at Louisiana State University and the $27,000,000 spent by the Alice and Erle Nye Academic Center at Texas A&M.[7] It is doubtful that many libraries could budget such large sums to create a personal librarian program; however, the kinds of services offered are often within the reach of library staff, if on a smaller scale. These schools provide tutors and dedicated spaces and make a concerted effort to meet their goals. A personal librarian program can do all of these things and already has a dedicated space, the library!

INFORMATION TECHNOLOGY SERVICES

As with academic support centers, library staff have both much to learn from and much to share with information technology professionals. In many ways the departmental goals of these professionals also seem to be intertwined. According to Andrea Coles and William Dougherty in *College and Research Libraries News*, "The interdependence between information science and information technology is inherent in the interplay of each field's related professions. If we use a loose definition of the term systems, we could consider the relationship between libraries and information technology departments as a system."[8] Indeed, many students do not differentiate between information technology services and the library when services are bundled. Each department or area has traditionally had the same explicit goal as libraries of providing resources to students in order to make them more successful. The increasing need for the personalization of services and the development of relationships has found its way into the provision of information technology services as well.

For example, technology help services are sometimes more tailored and personalized than in the past. If someone calls in to a help desk, he or she may get access to an information technology services staff member or student employee who will not only solve the current problem but also offer to be a personal contact for future problems or questions as well. An example from the University of North Carolina at Greensboro helps illustrate at least some of what is possible. This university has moved rapidly in recent years to provide more online courses or traditional courses that have online components. It can be very challenging for an institution to provide a high level of technology support not just to distance students but to faculty as well, especially adjunct faculty. The information technology services department at the university has solved this challenge by assigning adjuncts a dedicated professional to answer questions. The professionals communicate and assist faculty in a variety of ways. For example, the professional might send a customized e-mail to a faculty member containing a link to a Jing video tutorial that illustrates an answer to a question. These e-mails might even be customized to the extent of using the faculty member's name and referring to prior discussions in the voice-over component. Many libraries have begun the foray into online tutorials. Imagine, however, the possibility of creating instant customized and personal tutorials as part of a personal librarian program. Scalability may be a challenge, but what are the possibilities here?

Information technology services at the University of Minnesota created "Tech Stops." According to the university website, these are stations located at various places on campus that provide one-on-one assistance in setting up and using software and hardware. It is interesting to note that not all of the Tech Stop services are free. It is not clear how or if a minimal fee structure should be incorporated at all into a personal librarian program (I doubt we would want to charge for our services beyond what students are already paying in tuition). Still, the idea that one is able to walk into these stations and get personal assistance on a wide range of information technology–related issues from someone with whom they might form a longer term relationship is intriguing. One way that Tech Stops also seem to be marketed is through the frequent provision of small workshops. Indeed, the website encourages students to "Drop in For a Wee Byte of Learning."[9] Many of these ideas are not new (e.g., providing technical support), but the way they are packaged here is.

One other movement related to those discussed is the increased hiring of information technologists. Often these individuals possess a cross-section of skills related to both library and information technology services (although leaning more toward the latter). As more colleges and universities provide an ever greater online presence through course management systems, these individuals stand on the front lines often as quasi–personal assistants to faculty and staff. They provide workshops as well as point-of-need assistance. It seems fairly common for them to build long-lasting relationships with specific faculty who recognize their ability to provide exceptional support on everything from creating online quizzes to embedding videos in classes, connecting various university or college online resources and systems together (e.g., connecting library databases directly to course management pages).

While service is a mainstay of information technology services operations, the more typical method seems to be to provide answers online to commonly asked questions and to allow for other ways and means by which a student may acquire an answer to a question in a less than personal way. The emphasis seems to be more on a transactional encounter than on building long-term relationships between students and specific information technology services staff. It is interesting to consider if a personal librarian program would be adaptable to an information technology services environment. Perhaps information technology services staff could be assigned specific freshmen to reach out to in order to determine and assist with technology-related concerns? What if they were to partner with personal librarians? Could a student be assigned someone specific from both the library and information technology services?

CAREER SERVICES

The provision of professional assistance to students at institutions of higher education in finding jobs and launching their careers is not new. In recent years, however, college students and society have placed more significance on the need to graduate with specific job skills. Graduates need to hit the ground running. Career services can vary considerably from one school to the next. At Johnson & Wales University's Charlotte campus students have typically been assigned a specific or personal staff member to work with in the Experiential Education and Career Services department. This person is assigned based on the student's major. Experiential Education Coordinators establish relationships early on by going out of their way to meet students assigned to them. They attend orientation sessions, meet students in the dining center, and go to classes targeted at students studying specific majors. The interesting thing to note about these coordinators relative to our focus on relationships is that they need to also develop and maintain relationships with specific individuals at companies that might select students for internships or regular positions later on. Thus, their job is truly about long-term relationships in every way. Students are often assessed in depth to determine personality type, interests, and work habits. Regarding the advice she regularly gives to students, Jan-Marie Lanuzza, Experiential Education Coordinator, states, "No one size fits all. Everyone comes to you with different life situations."[10] Often, matching students and employers requires consideration of many personal factors. How can we apply this to a personal librarian program? Can we connect better with students regarding their long-term career goals? How can we reach out as aggressively as career service professionals have done? How can we help connect real-life job skills to what we do in a personal librarian program?

HEALTH SERVICES

Health services staff handle many challenges similar to those faced by library staff in accomplishing their mission. Some of the challenges relate to attempts to better personalize student services. With regard to mental health services in particular, one study identified four key reasons that students do not avail themselves of assistance: "They are embarrassed, they don't think counselors will help, they are unaware of the services or they think they can handle the issue on their own."[11] Jim Paterson, in an article advising health service professionals, emphasizes most especially the need to better market services for all these reasons. Furthermore, marketing of services must occur on a one-to-one basis. Patterson quotes David Diana, an experienced counselor and marketing expert, in stating, "It involves connecting with people personally at a grassroots level rather than with mass mailings or impersonal ads."[12] Again, there is a similar emphasis on building a personal connection through a personal librarian program. While mental health issues may be more difficult for a student to face, it is doubtful that any librarian would deny that many of the students who enter the library are embarrassed to ask for assistance or are simply unaware of what is available to them. A personal librarian program can break down these barriers. Some health services departments have found success in specializing in particular types of counseling or by targeting specific groups.[13] Yet again, we can see the similarity as library staff target specific groups of students and focus on building skills in specific areas, such as evaluating information or using information ethically.

Health services are, of course, multifaceted, go beyond mental health services, and branch into other areas as well. For example, Oregon State University developed a personalized program that targets student needs regarding diet and nutrition. According to its website, "Student Health offers one-on-one nutrition counseling to students who are trying to improve their diet. Consultations are provided by our Registered Dietitian. These services focus on dietary assessment and self-guided goal setting."[14] The site goes on to explain how students may establish a relationship and have regular meetings with their registered dietician to meet specific goals. It should be noted that this is just a sample of the impressive array of personalized services the Oregon State University Health Services department offers to deal with issues such as the use of alcohol, stress, sexual activity, and body image. In fact, what they refer to as "health coaching" seems to be their central focus.[15] Could we do this within the context of a personal librarian program? That is, could we, as they do at Oregon State University, assess student needs (in our case a wide array of information skills/needs) and then establish a series of follow-up meetings whereby we check in with students as they move closer toward meeting initially established goals? Could students be required to come prepared to the first session by considering their needs and writing in a journal? Could the students actually be involved in establishing a goal or goals that they will work toward with their personal librarian?

STUDENT AFFAIRS

Student affairs is without a doubt one of the biggest areas on campus in terms of interacting with students and impacting their overall college experience. The range of interactions can vary wildly from one campus to the next and depend on whether a student is a commuter or lives on campus. For those who live on campus, regular staff members, such as a hall director, or student staff members, such as resident assistants, have long assisted in a variety of ways. Often on-campus students are away from home for the first time, so the level and impact of interactions with these staff outside normal class times should never be underestimated. Many residence hall staff and student affairs staff in general have advanced degrees and experience that allows them to facilitate student needs and help students to mature, be successful in college, and ultimately graduate. Living off campus does not mean that students cannot be impacted by student affairs, especially as it relates to on-campus programming. While it is always more difficult to reach this group, careful and creative planning and thoughtful design can go a long way to making these students more connected.

The literature related to student affairs is both deep and vast. Chickering's often-cited study from 1969 has been a particularly central pillar of student affairs thinking for decades, especially as it relates to not just connecting with students but also helping them grow. According to Chickering, as typical college students seek to establish their identity, they struggle through seven vectors of development. Gatten believes we should apply knowledge of these vectors when we consider library-related student development initiatives:

1. Developing confidence
2. Managing emotions
3. Moving through autonomy toward interdependence
4. Developing more personal relationships
5. Establishing identity
6. Developing purpose
7. Developing integrity[16]

While some of these do not apply as obviously to a personal librarian program as others, a good program would definitely build students' confidence in their ability to find and use information, foster a greater sense of autonomy and relationship with information that is ultimately interdependent (with student as contributor), and help students develop personal relationships (by building on a professional model for communicating ideas) and the ability to utilize information in an ethical way.

Another scholar of noted influence in student affairs is Alexander Astin. In his seminal work *What Matters in College?*, Astin explored 140 student characteristics and 190 environmental characteristics to determine their impact on the development of thousands of students.[17] His intent was to answer the question, as his title would suggest, just what is it in the collegiate experience that makes the most difference for students and what does that mean for educators? In a nutshell, what he found was that students who were more engaged in the campus experienced more positive growth in areas such as intelligence, interpersonal skills, self-efficacy, and overall social awareness, among other things.[18] The implication was, and is, that the more connections students make and the more effort we and they make to stay involved, the more likely the student is to have a "successful" college experience. The connection between these findings and supporting the development of a personal librarian program is obvious. What is not obvious is why it has taken so long for library staff to figure this out!

It would take far too long here to recount the multitude of ways in which student affairs staff connect students to their campuses and utilize the aforementioned theories and findings. While they are focused on students living on campus, living–learning communities do provide us with a window or snapshot into how student affairs staff personalize the college experience. The basic description that follows is intended to help us consider two things: how we might better connect to students and, in a very practical way, how we might better partner with student affairs staff to enrich and improve our students' overall experiences. According to Merrily Dunn and Laura Dean, "In contemporary higher education, living learning communities are commonplace, difficult to define succinctly, and include a broad spectrum of configurations. Examples range from students living together in a residence hall community centered on a common theme to a fully integrated curriculum complemented by co-curricular activities designed to support, augment, and reinforce learning."[19] They then describe specific examples, including the Recreation and Fitness Living Learning Community at the College at Brockport, State University of New York, for students interested in careers in recreation and leisure; Miami University's Outdoor Leadership Living Learning Community, for students considering careers in outdoor recreation and education; and the University of Wisconsin at La Crosse's living–learning area, which focuses on sustainability issues as a component of outdoor recreation.[20] Indeed, they describe other examples as well, noting the commonalities and differences among the programs. According to Dunn and Dean, while these are recent examples, "learning communities are as old as higher education in the United States."[21] As proof, they mention the Experimental College created in 1927 at the University of Wisconsin by Alexander Meiklejohn. This college "brought students together with their advisors, living and working in Adams Hall. His goal was closer ties—intellectual and personal—among community members."[22] The connections to creating a personal librarian program are many. What are the possibilities of more fully integrating librarians into the student experience? Could we partner with a living–learning community or some other student activities program that more broadly connects with students? What ideas that have been tried in the past and written about in the literature could be revisited (clearly the Experimental College at the University of Wisconsin hints that there have been good ideas in the distant past that could be explored)?

ADMISSIONS AND STUDENT FINANCIAL SERVICES

Librarians tend to focus on the academic development of students as we target their needs *after* they arrive, but the personalization of services has typically begun long before that. Admissions officers and student financial services staff begin to develop relationships with students long before we come into contact with them. Customer relations management (CRM) is a key component of recruiting in the modern university or college. With a limited number of students to recruit from and the need to stay competitive, every college and university looks for an edge in this regard. Recruiting usually includes the implementation of specialized software that in many cases is integrated with other university and college systems. Some packages that admissions department staff use are Talisma at the University of Nebraska–Lincoln, PeopleSoft Enterprise Learning Solution at the University of Houston, and Jenzabar at Florida Southern College.[23] In a nutshell, what all of these systems do is enable a staff member in admissions or financial services to easily assist a student or potential student by accessing all of his or her information from a single platform. They are also much more than that, since they allow students to access and manipulate their information directly as well. However, their primary purpose is to make it easier for staff to assist students so that students can focus on the many other challenges associated with college instead of the mind boggling array of paperwork associated with entering and maintaining enrollment. According to the manufacturer of Talisma, "The best CRM solutions enable colleges and universities to expand their relationship management strategies at any pace and as far afield as they desire."[24] Although our focus in building a personal librarian program is on the human interaction, how can our systems help us? What special challenges or issues might we have as librarians with regard to privacy? Is there a way for us to better track our interactions with students such that we are able to help build better relationships and assist students in a more effective and efficient way?

The approach of CRM systems is, of course, rooted in customer relationship marketing. One study examined an experiment at two institutions where the need to better market and manage relationships with students led to an effort to empower admissions staff such that they could do some of the aspects of enrollment previously done only by student financial services officers. The authors of the study do admit that the smaller nature of these schools helped facilitate the experiment, so it may not work everywhere: "Small colleges with a manageable incoming class size have a unique opportunity to foster a relationship . . . with every new student."[25] Through training and restructuring, especially of admissions staffing, these schools significantly increased and improved the personal relationships that the students experienced with the institution before they even started classes! This was very beneficial for the colleges, as evidenced by increased enrollment. One school went from a three-year average conversion rate of 57.9 percent to 70.2 percent, and the other went from 41.8 percent to 54.3 percent (conversion rates indicate how many accepted students actually enrolled).[26] The hope is that these students will also feel more connected to the school and that they have someone to turn to once they arrive if they should need directional assistance. Another positive impact of this approach is that many students later referred to the staff member who assisted them by name.[27] Surely, this is the kind of connection we seek in any personal librarian program. Other questions this brief exploration of admissions and financial services raise are how soon is too soon for us to start building a relationship with students, and how might we expand our knowledge or better train library staff so that they can assist (even if only to give direction) on a wider range of student issues and needs?

CONCLUSION

We did not intend this exploration to be comprehensive. There are obviously many ways that colleges and universities are seeking to create better and deeper personal connections with students. A personal librarian program in this sense is just one arrow in the quiver. It is important for library staff attempting to implement and refine a personal librarian program to understand this. It is also important for these librarians to learn from the myriad ways by which the institution establishes and maintains contact with students. Some of these ideas and approaches could point to creative ways for improving student contact with the library and its staff.

NOTES

1. Komives and Woodard, *Student Services*, 336–337.
2. Reference and User Services Association, "Guidelines for Behavioral Performance."
3. Landsberger, "Academic Support Centers," 10.
4. Ibid.
5. Flaherty, interview by author.
6. Mapes, "You Need to Realize It in Yourself," 523.
7. Wolverton, Kelderman, and Moser, "Spending Plenty," A1–A2.
8. Coles and Dougherty, "Hang Together or Hang Separately," 110.
9. "Tech Stop."
10. Lanuzza, interview by author.
11. Paterson, "Right Medicine," 43.
12. Ibid.
13. Ibid., 45.
14. Student Health Services, "Nutrition."
15. Ibid.
16. Chickering as cited in Gatten, "Student Psychosocial and Cognitive Development," 157.
17. Astin, *What Matters in College?*, xvii.
18. Ibid., 365–395.
19. Dunn and Dean, "Together We Live and Learn," 12.
20. Ibid., 14–15.
21. Ibid., 13.
22. Ibid.
23. Gaska, "CRM Hits the Campus."
24. "Value of a Long-Term Investment in CRM."
25. Vander Schee, "Small College Enrollment Officer," 137.
26. Ibid., 141.
27. Ibid.

BIBLIOGRAPHY

Astin, Alexander. *What Matters in College?* San Francisco, CA: Jossey-Bass, 1993.

Coles, Andrea A., and William Dougherty. "Hang Together or Hang Separately." *College and Research Libraries News* 70, no. 2 (2009): 110–113.

Dunn, Merrily, and Laura Dean. "Together We Live and Learn: Living–Learning Communities as Integrated Curricular Experiences." *Schole: A Journal of Leisure Studies and Recreation Education* 1, no. 28 (2013): 11–23.

Flaherty, Susan. Interview by author. Charlotte, NC, July 10, 2013.

Gaska, C. L. "CRM Hits the Campus." *University Business* 6, no. 11 (2003): 28–32.

Gatten, Jeffrey N. "Student Psychosocial and Cognitive Development: Theory to Practice in Academic Libraries." *Reference Services Review* 32, no. 2 (2004): 157–163.

Komives, Susan, and Dudley Woodard. *Student Services: A Handbook for the Profession.* San Francisco, CA: Jossey-Bass, 1996.

Landsberger, Joe. "Academic Support Centers: Quo Vadis?" *TechTrends: Linking Research and Practice to Improve Learning* 49, no. 4 (2005): 8–11.

Lanuzza, Jan-Marie. Interview by author. Charlotte, NC, July 23, 2013.

Mapes, Aimee C. "You Need to Realize It in Yourself: Positioning, Improvisation, and Literacy." *Journal of Adolescent and Adult Literacy* 54, no. 7 (2011): 515–524.

Paterson, Jim. "The Right Medicine." *Counseling Today* 53, no. 1 (2010): 42–45.

Reference and User Services Association. "Guidelines for Behavioral Performance of Reference Service and Information Service Providers." American Library Association. Last updated May 28, 2013. www.ala.org/rusa/resources/guidelines/guidelinesbehavioral.

Stassen, Martha L. A. 2003. "Student Outcomes: The Impact of Varying Living–Learning Community Models." *Research in Higher Education* 44, no. 5: 581–613.

Student Health Services. "Nutrition." Oregon State University. Accessed April 13, 2013. http://studenthealth.oregonstate.edu/nutrition.

"The Value of a Long-Term Investment in CRM for Higher Education." Campus Management. Accessed May 20, 2014. www.talisma.com/products/White%20Papers/Whitrepaper_Value_of_Long_Term_Investment_in_CRM_for_HE.pdf.

"Tech Stop." University of Minnesota. Last updated February 18, 2013. www.oit.umn.edu/tech-stop/index.htm.

Vander Schee, Brian A. "The Small College Enrollment Officer: Relationship Marketing at Work." *Journal of Marketing for Higher Education* 20, no. 1 (2010): 135–143.

Wolverton, Brad, Eric Kelderman, and Kate Moser. "Spending Plenty So Athletes Can Make the Grade." *Chronicle of Higher Education* 55, no. 2 (2008): A1–A23.

DAVID JEWELL

8
The Faculty Perspective on Personal Librarians

THERE ARE PROGRAMS THAT TRY TO INTEGRATE LIBRARIANS and faculty. There are also barriers and hurdles that prevent librarians and faculty from working well with each other.[1] The personal librarian program at Johnson & Wales University tried to avoid potential issues by aligning the common goals of librarians and faculty, allowing faculty choice in the level of librarian integration, and using effective and consistent communication.

Alignment of the personal librarian program goals with the faculty goals was prioritized.[2] There was an intentional emphasis on how the personal librarian program could help with student achievement of both course outcomes/objectives and increased quality of research papers. In addition, the program could reduce the burden on faculty of teaching information literacy and research methods. Faculty buy-in should not be surprising if one can potentially improve the quality of student papers and reduce the workload.

Faculty teaching ENG 1020 (English Composition) were specifically targeted to integrate the personal librarian program into their courses. Faculty are notoriously independent.[3] With this in mind, the program was designed to give faculty a choice in the range of participation options—from a minimal integration to a more robust integration. The minimum level of participation requested that the faculty e-mail the students in their course the name and contact information of the students' personal librarians. The upper range of participation included adding the personal librarians into discussion board chats on ulearn (Blackboard), creating research assignments in conjunction with them, allowing them to visit the classrooms, and more.

It is worth repeating that faculty are fiercely independent,[4] and the framing of any program that is requesting access to faculty courses must be positioned around faculty choice and common goals (improved student outcomes and time release rather than time consumption). Alignment of goals and providing faculty choices in the level of intervention are important in determining the success of a program that combines librarians and faculty. Without effective communication, however, any program can struggle.

COMMUNICATION AND TIMELINE

Any new program needs to have frequent and effective communications among its participants to be successful. The personal librarian program at Johnson & Wales University was no exception. Most communications regarding the personal librarian program emphasized the alignment of the faculty's and the librarians' goals, including increased student success and faculty choice.

At the closing of the 2011–2012 academic school year (May 2012), a full three months before the fall term rollout, the personal librarian program was discussed in Arts and Sciences meetings and in more detail in meetings held exclusively by the English faculty at Johnson & Wales. The following month (June 2012), when most faculty members were not teaching over the summer, communication continued by e-mail with a flyer sent to all English faculty. The e-mail outlined the choices of course integration with the personal librarian program from minimal to full. The flyer design made an analogy between a personal trainer and a personal librarian.

Johnson & Wales faculty participate in an orientation one week before the fall term begins, generally during the last week of August. Just before the faculty orientation, another personal librarian program communication was sent out to the Arts and Sciences faculty. During the orientation, the program was introduced to all faculty, regardless of discipline. Other disciplines, in addition to English, became interested in the potential of the program for their courses.

During the fall term of the 2012–2013 academic year, all of the ENG 1020 (English Composition) faculty incorporated the personal librarian program in some way into their course. The same is true for the winter term. The winter term also had an additional e-mail and flyer communication. This communication focused on some of the successes in the fall term with quotes from students. At the end of the winter term, ENG 1020 faculty were given a survey regarding the new initiative. Six of the six full-time faculty completed the personal librarian program survey.

A faculty in-service session during the spring term (March 15, 2013) highlighted Live Chat, an additional way for faculty to integrate the program into their courses. Through Live Chat librarians can interact with students and assist faculty. The option garnered attention, and the college chair of Arts and Sciences sent an additional e-mail to all Arts and Sciences faculty on March 21, 2013. It encouraged faculty to add the Live Chat option to the online portion of their courses. The same personal librarian program survey that was completed in the winter term was offered again at the end of the spring term. Four of five full-time faculty teaching ENG 1020 completed the spring term survey.

FACULTY RESPONSES: THE PERSONAL LIBRARIAN PROGRAM SURVEY

The personal librarian program survey comprised six questions—one multiple choice question, three Likert scale questions, and two open-ended questions. The one multiple choice question (1) qualified the faculty member for the survey. The three Likert scale questions (2, 3, and 6) captured quantitative data, and the two open-ended questions (4 and 5) captured qualitative information.

Personal Librarian Program Survey

Question 1: Incorporated the personal librarian program in some way into my English course in the winter (or spring) term of the 2012–2013 academic year.

Question 2: Incorporated the personal librarian program in a meaningful way into my English course.

Question 3: The personal librarian program helped my students on outcomes and/or objectives for the course, such as better research papers.

Question 4: What could the personal librarian program do to better help your students?

Question 5: What could you do to better incorporate the personal librarian program into your English course?

Question 6: What is your general opinion of the personal librarian program?

The same survey was used at the end of the following winter and spring terms, and the same English faculty were asked to complete the survey at the end of each term. Six of the six full-time English faculty teaching ENG 1020 in the winter and four of the five full-time English faculty teaching ENG 1020 in the spring completed the survey. All of the faculty answered that they incorporated the personal librarian program in some way into their English course during the term, thus qualifying them for the survey.

Quantitative Results

QUESTION 2

I incorporated the personal librarian program in a meaningful way into my English course.

	Winter term	Spring term
Strongly agree	16.67% (1)	50% (2)
Agree	83.33% (5)	25% (1)
Neither agree nor disagree	0%	25% (1)
Disagree	0%	0%
Strongly disagree	0%	0%

Thoughts and Discussion

From the winter term to the spring term, there is a positive shift (one-fifth to one-half) from "agree" to "strongly agree." There is also a negative shift (zero to one-quarter) from "agree" to "neutral." We believe this data suggests an overall positive shift for the faculty in relation to the personal librarian program. Furthermore, this question is asked about how the faculty member delivered the personal librarian program in their course. Thus, it was a secondary measurement compared to the student success results.

QUESTION 3

The personal librarian program helped my students on outcomes and/or objectives for the course, such as better research papers.

Thoughts and Discussion

Question 3 addressed a core issue with faculty, helping with student success and course outcomes/objectives. Zero faculty in the winter term would "strongly agree" that the personal librarian program helped with student outcomes. After the spring term, however, one of four faculty would "strongly

	Winter term	Spring term
Strongly agree	0%	25% (1)
Agree	66.67% (4)	50% (2)
Neither agree nor disagree	16.67% (1)	0%
Disagree	16.67% (1)	25% (1)
Strongly disagree	0%	0%

agree" that the personal librarian program helped with student outcomes. Furthermore, after both terms, at least half of the faculty did "agree" that the personal librarian program helped with student outcomes. The general trend from the winter term to the spring term was a positive shift.

Qualitative Results

QUESTION 4

What could the personal librarian program do to better help your students?

Winter Term

Generally, faculty feedback was supportive of the librarians and the personal librarian program. Examples of comments include "It seems to be working pretty well" and "I have no suggestions for improvement." One faculty member mentioned the high level of connection by the librarian assigned to the course:

> The librarian that I worked with was added to my ulearn section so that they were able to communicate with students via course announcements. In addition, this individual also visited my classroom where they were introduced to students in person.

Spring Term

Once again, the general sentiment for question 4 was that the librarians were doing a lot for both information literacy and the personal librarian program. For example, one faculty member stated:

> I don't think they could do much more. They were available, they gave me a link to post a live chat space on my class ulearn page, they conducted the library module class, and they emailed my students directly to introduce the program.

In addition, there is evidence that the efforts of the university librarians were potentially motivating for the faculty:

> I think that I could do more next term by encouraging my students to
> seek out their help more than they did this term. I think the students
> don't see a need for the personal librarian until the final week of classes
> when essays are due. What I plan to do next term is incorporate the
> librarians in more of a direct way: actually have the students go to them
> for help and feedback for at least one assignment (probably finding and
> citing sources).

Other faculty statements suggest that the librarians are fulfilling their commitment to the personal librarian program at Johnson & Wales. One faculty member mentioned, "The current information literacy sessions that the personal librarians conduct are *perfect* for my needs."

The faculty also recognize the limitations of the personal librarian program regarding less controlled factors, such as student effort and student engagement:

> I think the idea of the personal librarian is great. The problem, how-
> ever, continues to be one of student engagement in the program. The
> librarian came to my ENG 1020 class once this term, and I thought that
> personal connection might make them more inclined to visit the library.
> This wasn't the case, though. I was told that one student visited the
> librarian during spring term.

QUESTION 5
What could you do to better incorporate the personal librarian program into your English course?

Winter Term

The responses to question 5 were solid suggestions and mostly focused on the faculty members: "There could be more collaboration between library staff and faculty to integrate the program better into the individual classes," "Continue to work closely with the librarian," "I will continue to work with the librarian to redesign some of the research projects," "Advertising/showing the value-added aspect of the personal librarian and the IL [information literacy] sessions is the best thing I can think of to do," and "Use more database types of resources."

Spring Term

The feedback to question 5 revolves around assignments: "Incorporate academic research into papers throughout the course (versus just at the end of the term)" and "I could require that students visit the librarian as a part of their grade; I'm not sure if that is feasible, though." An interesting comment from one faculty member might suggest a more tailored approach for the personal librarian program at Johnson & Wales: "Not every student needs the extra attention and I'm not sure that the librarian has the time to speak to that number of students." Perhaps at-risk students could be identified by the faculty member and then directed to the librarian.

What is your general opinion of the personal librarian program?

	Winter term	Spring term
Very favorable	16.67% (1)	75% (3)
Favorable	50% (3)	0%
Neutral	16.67% (1)	25% (1)
Unfavorable	16.67% (1)	0%
Very unfavorable	0%	0%

Thoughts and Discussion

Question 6 shows a marked positive shift in the general opinion of the personal librarian program from the winter term to the spring term. We find this shift to be the result of frequent and effective communications, strong effort by the librarians to provide value for both the faculty member (time and outcomes) and the students (resources and outcomes), and the importance for the program to allow for flexibility.

One can see the clear and obvious benefits to faculty and students that result from participation in a personal librarian program. I highly recommend that other institutions implement a similar program.

NOTES

1. McGuinness, "What Faculty Think."
2. Asher et al., "Feeling Like a Third Wheel?"
3. Jenkins, "How Are Professors Like Cats?"
4. Ibid.

BIBLIOGRAPHY

Asher, Andrew, Susan Miller, Mariana Regalado, and Maura A. Smale. "Feeling Like a Third Wheel? Leveraging Faculty–Student–Librarian Relationships for Student Success." Poster presented at the ACRL 2011 National Conference, Philadelphia, PA. www.erialproject.org/wp-content/uploads/2011/04/ACRL2011poster.pdf.

Jenkins, Rob. "How Are Professors Like Cats? Let Me Count the Ways." *Chronicle of Higher Education*, April 12, 2010. http://chronicle.com/article/How-Are -Professors-Like-Cat/65032.

McGuinness, Claire. "What Faculty Think—Exploring the Barriers to Information Literacy Development in Undergraduate Education." *Journal of Academic Librarianship* 32, no. 6 (2006): 573–582.

RICHARD MONIZ

9

Best Practices and a Checklist for Personal Librarians

WHILE NUMEROUS DETAILED STUDIES OF BEST PRACTICES exist for any number of library services, from collection development to information literacy, such is not the case for personal librarian programs. There is information, and much, if not most, of what is available has hopefully found its way into the pages of this book. Yet, there is no definitive study of best practices for the type of program that we are proposing. We suspect there are many reasons for this. Programs defined as "personal librarian" are certainly not common. We have found that many other programs do present some of the features of a personal librarian program without being specifically named as such. The concept of personal librarian is also fairly new and represents a fundamentally different approach to librarianship. Finally, many personal librarian programs, including the one several of the authors of this text are engaged in, are still evolving. Thus, there does not exist the kind of concrete guidance that we have in other, more established areas of librarianship. That said, we feel it worth the effort, after exploring the topic as much as we have, to identify and describe what we feel are best practices in this regard. Our hope is that this review will help you as you develop your program and ideas. We have also included a brief "checklist" to follow that can get you up and going right away.

WEBPAGES THAT PERSONALIZE THE LIBRARY

In times past, when one referred to a library, it would always conjure images of a physical space. That has changed dramatically over the past twenty years, and the pace of change seems to be quickening all the time. At the most extreme end of the spectrum, students enrolled in pure distance education programs may not ever even set foot in a physical library at their school. In traditional and blended programs, students often equate the library with the library's website as well. That is, the virtual trumps the physical. The importance of a library's web presence, therefore, cannot be overstated. As such, the need to humanize and personalize the site becomes imperative when implementing a personal librarian program. The programs at Yale University, Barnard College at Columbia University, and Texas Tech University, to name a few, all do this well by providing profiles of personal librarians. For example, librarians at Yale's Harvey Cushing/John K. Whitney Medical Library include pictures, office locations, and contact information on their website. Barnard College at Columbia University does the same while also allowing librarians to create their own research start page with recommended links to databases, LibGuides, and other resources. Texas Tech University provides contact information, pictures, office locations, and links. Additionally, the library website provides students with a directory where they can find out which personal librarian is attached to their particular area of study. Many other institutions follow this best practice as well.

A recent study by Pampaloni and Bird highlights the general importance of librarians being more proactive and personal through the library website. They note, "A digital branch recreates not only the functional features of a library but the relational aspects as well."[1] Sadly, this study also indicates that libraries could do a much better job at fostering relationships through their websites. It is a small thing in some respects, but it would go a long way toward helping us enhance the student experience![2]

VIDEOS: HUMANIZE THE LIBRARIANS
AND FILL SPECIFIC USER NEEDS

Texas Tech University began filming personal librarians on a voluntary basis in November 2010. This can be seen as the next most logical step beyond providing static pictures on the library's website. The videos can then be attached to the website or pushed out to students through e-mail. The intent of the short videos was to show who the librarians were, even to the extent of including their personal interests and passions outside the library.[3] Again, this seems like a logical progression from posting pictures to a library website.

Where best practices regarding the use of short videos shows still more promise is in the ability to meet individual user needs through targeted tutorials. The technology to quickly create custom videos for research-related topics and then push them out to students is almost limitless. At the University of North Carolina at Greensboro, as noted earlier in this book, adjunct faculty are given access to a technology professional who can assist them on a personal basis. It is not uncommon for an information technology services professional associated with what is referred to as the 6-Tech Online service to make a short video for a specific purpose, for example, to show and explain how to utilize Blackboard, the popular online course management system. While there might be some scalability issues with utilizing this approach in a more widespread fashion, the potential exists for sending a student a voice-over video demonstrating how to search a specific database or how to click on certain tools and use them within a given database. The personal librarian might even refer to the students by name in the video!

ASSIGNING PERSONAL LIBRARIANS TO A SPECIFIC DEPARTMENT

Personal librarian programs assign librarians in a wide variety of ways. In many cases, the decision over how librarians are assigned is determined by practical limitations and possibilities, such as the size of the institution, the number of librarians, or the goals of the program. It seems clear, though, that there are particular advantages to assigning personal librarians to the specific areas of study with which they are familiar. For example, at Barnard College, librarians are able to utilize their previous expertise as liaisons to the faculty of a given department as they are then assigned to serve as personal librarians to the students in that same department.[4] The connection to specific knowledge and expertise is obvious. The challenge with this model is that it does not necessarily work everywhere. For instance, if the point where personal librarians intersect with students is in a mixed-major English class, such a model becomes impractical. In this case, a personal librarian, while still assisting the student, can serve as a bridge for introducing the student to other librarians as well, perhaps even one associated with liaison responsibilities in the student's chosen program of study.

UTILIZING E-MAIL TO CONNECT WITH STUDENTS

E-mail is an effective tool in a variety of ways for communicating with students. Good practice seems to include contacting students at the very beginning of the term before attempting to meet them in person. This is the first opportunity to make students aware of what a personal librarian can (or cannot) do for them. Additional e-mails at a later time can remind students about their personal librarian's availability to assist. These reminders can be strategically timed based on knowledge of the research needs students will have at a specific time in a specific class. It has also been suggested that librarians could provide additional information that they know will be of use to students, such as reminders about course registration for a future semester, projects or events occurring on campus that relate to a specific course or a particular student's interests, or other messages that could encourage a student to pursue further research opportunities.[5] It remains a balancing act, of course. One does not want to be seen as spamming students but rather communicating information that is of particular use to *that* student. Pioneers of the personal librarian program at the University of Richmond were especially careful to make sure they were not perceived as "bugging" students.[6] Still, experience seems to indicate that more is better than less in this regard.

HOLDING PERSONAL LIBRARIAN OFFICE HOURS

Faculty have held office hours for students in the United States since colonial times. Librarians have also frequently recognized the need for meeting with students one-on-one as well. Research consultations, especially with graduate students and faculty, are not new. Although the way that office hours are contextualized through a personal librarian program may be different, librarians have known the benefits of this practice for some time. According to Susan Avery, Jim Hahn, and Melissa Zilic in 2008, "those providing office hours service find it much easier to get a student started on their research. . . . This setting also provides the ability to focus on research as a process [and] the students attending office hours generally receive a more holistic research experience."[7] Clearly, many institutions see holding office hours as a best practice in general, but it seems to fit especially well with the personal librarian concept. We should note that office hours do not preclude the necessity of juggling students if more than one arrives at the same time. The kind of triage that librarians are familiar with from work at the reference desk can help alleviate some of this challenge by determining which needs can be met more quickly than others, getting one student started with the research process, moving on to another student, and then coming back to the student one started assisting to check on progress.[8] As Avery and colleagues noted, "As our students change so, too, must our service models. . . . Clearly a 'one size fits all' model will not meet their needs."[9] A personal librarian takes as a premise this key truth and proceeds from there.

MARKET APPROPRIATELY, MARKET WELL, MARKET ALL THE TIME

It almost goes without saying that the library needs to effectively market a personal librarian program. Librarians should know this almost intuitively in that they have historically needed to consider marketing with all prior services and resources. Students cannot take advantage of resources and opportunities of which they are unaware. It is not uncommon for surveys and focus groups to convey the desire of students for services and resources that already exist! One study of personal librarian programs indicated that marketing fell short of ideal. In a follow-up survey, students indicated that "the library needs to provide a better description of the program and its intent for students."[10] Getting the word out about a personal librarian program should be multifaceted and constantly under way. Students should hear about it during admissions tours, during orientation and registration periods, as part of their introduction to appropriate classes, in the hallways, and so forth. Faculty are also key partners and should be made aware and frequently reminded of just what a personal librarian can do through e-mails, librarians visiting faculty meetings, and orientation activities. The library could also produce brochures, flyers, and posters, provide giveaways, and sponsor events—all intended to increase awareness of the library's personal librarian program.

WORK AS A TEAM

Librarians need to work as a team in order to make a personal librarian program effective. Again, this practice relates not just to this type of program and service but to others that have preceded it as well. While the relationship sought is one whereby a specific student connects with a specific librarian, the process of building and improving a personal librarian program requires constant interaction among library staff. By sharing what works, what does not work, and what possibilities remain unexplored, librarians can create a vibrant program that fits their library and institution. As we emphasize in this book, there is no one-size-fits-all program. Rather, it is up to librarians "on the ground" to determine the effectiveness of different approaches within a specific context.

LEARN FROM OUTSIDE THE LIBRARY

Many ideas can be taken from outside the library world and adapted to libraries and a personal librarian program, as we have exemplified throughout. We have all heard of personal trainers at the gym. What do they do well that we do not? What other ideas have we not caught on to? Technology presents an almost limitless array of possibilities. How do we plug in to our students and add the online connection that many of them feel comfortable with? We should always be on the lookout for ideas, whether we are shopping online or standing in line at Target. Again, what is being done well elsewhere, and what is not? Best practices should imply constant innovation on our part!

A PERSONAL LIBRARIAN CHECKLIST

What follows is not intended to be prescriptive. Instead, it is a general checklist that can be adapted and changed based on your specific needs. It is up to you to decide which pieces work for you.

- [ ] **Identify the target population.** This could constitute all freshmen, all students in a given major, or any other appropriate designation.

- [ ] **Determine what your personal librarian program will focus on.** This involves a *lot* of staff discussion, considering feedback from students and faculty, and communicating with other areas of the college or university. What do you hope to accomplish?

- [ ] **Determine how your personal librarian program will be implemented.** This involves asking many follow-up questions, such as:
  - [ ] How will students be initially assigned and contacted?
  - [ ] How often will students be contacted thereafter?
  - [ ] How many live or in-person sessions will these students have with their personal librarian?
  - [ ] How will the personal librarian meet with students? For example, will there be office hours, appointments, both?
  - [ ] Who will schedule the in-class sessions, and how will they be recorded? For example, will it be done the same way that other instruction is documented, or is something different or special required?

- [ ] **Market your program.** This involves the whole array of options discussed for contacting students and faculty and getting the word out. It is especially important that the librarians work as a team to create a positive impression and aura of the personal librarian initiative.

☐ **Assess the program.** Determine how you will assess the program, exploring not just awareness of the program but also impact on student learning.

☐ **Meet with library staff to determine changes.** At the end of each semester or school year attempt to make changes based on what has been learned. The focus always needs to remain on how a personal librarian is helping individual students become more successful.

NOTES

1. Pampaloni and Bird, "Building Relationships," 6.
2. Ibid.
3. Henry, Vardeman, and Syma, "Reaching Out."
4. Freedman, "Implementing a Personal Librarian Program," 12.
5. Nann, "Personal Librarians," 22.
6. Dillon, "Personal Librarian Program," 12.
7. Avery, Hahn, and Zilic, "Beyond Consultation," 196.
8. Ibid., 203.
9. Ibid., 205.
10. Spak and Glover, "Personal Librarian Program," 23.

BIBLIOGRAPHY

Avery, Susan, Jim Hahn, and Melissa Zilic. "Beyond Consultation: A New Model for Librarian's Office Hours." *Public Services Quarterly* 4, no. 3 (2008): 187–206.

Dillon, Cy. "The Personal Librarian Program at the University of Richmond: An Interview with Lucretia McCulley." *Virginia Libraries* 57, no. 3 (2011): 11–12.

Freedman, Jenna. "Implementing a Personal Librarian Program for Students and Faculty at Barnard College." *The Unabashed Librarian* 157 (2011): 11–13.

Henry, Cynthia L., Kimberly K. Vardeman, and Carrye K. Syma. "Reaching Out: Connecting Students to Their Personal Librarian." *Reference Services Review* 40, no. 3 (2012): 396–407.

Nann, John B. "Personal Librarians." *AALL Spectrum* 14, no. 8 (2010): 22.

Pampaloni, Andrea, and Nora Bird. "Building Relationships through a Digital Branch Library: Finding the Community in Community College Library Web Sites." *Community College Journal of Research and Practice* (in press): citations from prepublication copy.

Spak, Judy M., and Janis G. Glover. "The Personal Librarian Program: An Evaluation of a Cushing/Whitney Medical Library Outreach Initiative." *Medical References Services Quarterly* 26, no. 4 (2007): 15–25.

JOE ESHLEMAN

10
The Future of the
Personal Librarian

P REDICTING, MUCH LESS GUESSING, THE FUTURE OFTEN TURNS
out to be an exercise in futility. Even present trends can be quickly superseded by technological changes, which means that current situations themselves can be moving targets. Such is the ever-changing world in which we live.
Despite this, it can be advantageous and even enlightening to attempt to foresee impending events. At minimum, thinking about the possible directions in
which personal librarian programs and librarianship that is focused on relationships will move can shed light on the mission of librarians and library
priorities. This final chapter provides an overview of the various and creative
ways in which librarians are interacting with those they come in contact with
and some conjecture on directions yet to come based on emerging trends.

LIBRARIANS INTERACTING AND CONNECTING

Numerous exhortations throughout this book emphasize the benefits of starting and maintaining a personal librarian program. At the core of the appeals

is the notion that whatever format is used—social media, embedded librarianship, or a personal librarian or similarly named program—librarians need to let students know who they are and what they can do. Although the basic concept of reaching out to students appears quite rudimentary, it seems that librarians sometimes struggle with directed social encounters and approachability. When contemplating the mission of an academic library or, more accurately, when speaking to most academic librarians about it, at core would be the question/goal, "How do we influence the academic and future success of students?" It would appear on face value that one easy answer to this question is to get to know students and form consistent supportive relationships. If the future of libraries involves an increased emphasis on personalized, meaningful, and dedicated service, then an increased awareness of and focus on this aspect should be considered.

Steven Bell says that one way to develop a meaningful library experience is to move from the role of gatekeeper to one of gate-opener:

> Our future may depend on our ability to differentiate what libraries offer and what library workers contribute to communities. The library profession should consider an alternate vision for our future: the library worker as gate-opener. In that role we shift from a focus on creating access to resources to creating meaningful relationships with community members—both those who use and those who don't use our libraries.[1]

He continues with this idea in the form of an example:

> [A] librarian spoke up and explained how students came by her office seeking assistance with research; nothing that unusual, but she related how that made the students feel good about having someone provide them with personal, caring help. From her perspective, that was how she created meaning in their lives. My observation was that *she* was the library experience; the user community derived meaning from her support. She didn't create or give 'stuff'; she delivered a meaningful experience. The profession's new mandate is to capture the essence of that experience and design it into the totality of library organization.[2]

It is easy to see how a well-designed and robust personal librarian program can help to achieve meaningful library experiences.

Another way in which librarians can create a personalized library experience with meaning to users is to get to know their community better. Bell feels as though the role evolved because "we needed to get out into the community and make the library not about the resources and the technology but about us."[3] Community-led librarianship is currently associated primarily with public libraries, yet the core concepts can be used to some extent in an academic setting and, again, map to personal librarian tenets. Starting from the idea that some people in a community do not use the library and then reaching out to those who might feel excluded, community-led library work "is a process in which relationship building is of prime importance because it allows greater understanding of the person or community so that the library can work collaboratively with the person or community, or take other suitable action."[4]

Perhaps a future goal for academic libraries, and one that personal librarians can be at the forefront of achieving, is gaining a greater understanding of the community that is being served as well as those who are not (and inviting them in). Certainly the idea of focusing on patrons is not a novel concept, and many initiatives are already in place that accomplish this; in fact, the corollary idea of creating value for the academic library is a worthwhile current and continuing topic. The notion that library advocates on campus create value combined with the knowledge that the need for library resources is in a constant state of competition with technological advances would seem to point in the direction of enterprises that target persistent and personalized student and librarian relations. Or, as John Pateman and Ken Williment state it:

> A community development approach is based on creating meaningful and sustained relationships with local communities, while acknowledging that the community is the expert on its members' own needs. Library staff become listeners rather than tellers, and staff and community co-produce library services. Community-led work is not prescriptive, which is a major strength, as it is highly adaptable and applicable to all contexts and communities which librarians are working in, or could be working in.[5]

As a parallel to the ERIAL study referenced in chapter 3, an awareness of the community by the librarians as well as an awareness of the librarians by the community can lead to beneficial connections and collaborations.

The understanding that some of the changes required to implement a personal librarian program can be difficult for the librarian has been touched on earlier in this book, particularly in chapter 3. Although a number of the chapters in this book address the various ways in which libraries and other institutions attempt to design and implement personalized service and also form relationships with patrons, there is a limit to, as well as a happy medium for, such initiatives. Time management issues, scheduling hurdles, new responsibilities, and even physical changes, such as jettisoning the reference desk, can all occur. In the Research Libraries UK study that delved into the issue of making library changes in "RLUK Redefining the Research Library Model," the writers surmised that services and staff will "require qualities of flexibility, an outward-looking perspective and a wide range of new skills. The baseline is a more dynamic, pro-active, customized and communicative approach from professional librarians than many researchers may be used to encountering."[6] Therefore, there can be a readjustment for librarians as well as patrons.

For the students in an academic environment, aggressive library marketing and continual unwanted communications can create a mixed reaction. While it is good for students to know that research support is available, it can be tricky for a librarian to walk the tightrope between assisting them and nagging them. Additionally, the old adage that "you can lead a horse to water but you can't make it drink" comes into play here. Various reasons students may not use librarians for research help have been discussed; one that has not been touched on is the idea of students seeing research as a task they would rather accomplish themselves, without aid. This line of thought can also create a type of anxiety for the librarian, wherein it can be difficult to find the right balance between being overbearing or aloof to a student. Another consideration is the idea of hand-holding versus creating an independent researcher. Although all of these elements are part and parcel of everyday librarian life, they can be amplified in a personal librarian setting but often offset with a balanced methodology.

ATTITUDES, ENVIRONMENTS, AND APPROACHES

Despite the simplification of personal librarian programs as boiling down to connections and collaborations, libraries have found unique and creative ways to exemplify these conceptions. With the advent of makerspaces, many libraries have moved from a resource and collection oriented stance to one that includes a focus on innovation and creation. Also moving from a former role that was more service oriented, librarians have also progressed to positions as forward-thinking collaborators. Because of the relative newness of makerspaces, there has been a great deal of discussion about their place in the library. Put bluntly, makerspaces are creative places for making and involve a much more "hands-on" approach to physical and virtual resources than is commonly seen in libraries. Makerspaces can be described this way:

> Makerspaces are collaborative learning environments where people come together to share materials and learn new skills. . . . [M]akerspaces are not necessarily born out of a specific set of materials or spaces, but rather a mindset of community partnership, collaboration, and creation.[7]

While there is an obvious participatory nature to makerspaces, one component of them achieves some of the motives of personal librarian programs, for example, heightening the role of the librarian and forming a working relationship with those who make. New trends in libraries can initially be dismissed as new twists on old ideas, and some view makerspaces as simply a new way to define how libraries have always been engaging patrons and helping them to create new ideas and materials. Yet the connection with emerging technologies seems to touch all innovations in the library, which can be seen as a major break from past initiatives. Librarians have also branched out in recent years to hold workshops on a number of topics, such as interpersonal skills, interviewing, and creating a mindful campus, that might have been thought of as being out of their purview in previous years. Of course, in a general sense, the creation of any type of work done by students, whether it is considered academic work or not, can help to fulfill the goal of the library. As Barbara Fister puts it, libraries, are for "helping [students] discover within themselves the ability to create new knowledge; to develop the skills that will not only help them recognize authority, but to become, themselves, authors of the world they're stepping into when they graduate."[8]

Another possibility for libraries that is currently implemented in a limited way and puts an interesting twist on some of the aspects of the personal librarian program is the Human Library Project. The University of Alberta's Augustana Human Library is "an initiative in which people called 'Readers' who want to learn about a specific topic 'check out' people called 'Human Books' for an hour of conversation."[9] Based on the original Human Library, which was started in Denmark, the idea behind this type of library is to "promote dialogue, reduce prejudices and encourage understanding."[10] It accomplishes this task as "Visitors to a Human Library are given the opportunity to speak informally with 'people on loan'; this latter group being extremely varied in age, sex and cultural background."[11] This type of library is usually set up for a short time, perhaps as a weekend event, although there are cases where it is a more continuous venture. The Human Library Project also realizes some of the aims of the aforementioned community-led library.

Daniel Pink has written several books that deal with the changing nature of the world and the workplace. In *A Whole New Mind: Why Right-Brainers Will Rule the Future*, he outlines the important skills that will be needed for the direction in which the world is moving. Pink contends that, moving forward, three important distinctions will occur that will give people advantages in the workplace. If someone overseas cannot do your job for a cheaper wage, or if a computer cannot do it faster, or if you are offering something that satisfies the nonmaterial, transcendent desires of an abundant age, then you hold an advantage over those who cannot meet these future requirements.[12] While there might be some debate about and lack of control over the first two prerequisites, the third one can be met with a good personal librarian program. A personal and dedicated relationship that deals primarily with an individual's needs is difficult, if not impossible, to duplicate.

Although great strides continue to be made with personalized computer assistants, such as Apple's Siri, a consistent and multidimensional research relationship is, for now, a province of librarians. Perhaps some type of software that recognizes when the user is doing research and notifies a librarian for proactive help would be of use in competition with a personalized computer assistant; currently, aware and directed chat software such as Zopim Live Chat and SnapEngage Live Chat on webpages accomplishes some of this design. Many of the "librarian replacers" of the past have not fully superseded the wide variety of personalized and dedicated services that librarians offer. Discussions on how long the services of librarians, in particular reference services, will be needed due to advances in search engines and automated assistants continue to occur. Often the fateful predictions of the end of librarians and libraries are attached to outdated conceptions and uninformed opinions of what librarians do and what is available in modern libraries. Of note here is that attempting to inform constituents about the role and services of librarians is at the heart of personal librarian programs. As Andy Barnett states it, "The assistance supplied by actual humans is another killer app."[13]

Jim Neal's ideas on the radical collaboration potential of libraries touch on the avoidance of institutional redundancies, especially collections.[14] This idea can also be applied to services such as library instruction, which is evidenced by sharing of tutorials and library instruction resources on websites such as the ANimated Tutorial Sharing Project (http://ants.wikifoundry.com). When it comes to personal librarians and radical collaboration, perhaps libraries can share collected experiences and best practices (which are addressed in chapter 9) but also use technology and pool resources to help create continuously available personal librarians for all. Adjacently, perhaps a forum for such a collaborative venture would be a Massive Open Online Course (MOOC).

Chapter 4 discussed embedded librarians and showed how distance learning environments afford the ability to personalize librarian efforts in an online class. While MOOCs can currently be considered to be a form of larger (massive) and more accessible (open) online courses, other aspects differentiate the two and how librarians, whether embedded or personal, can work within them. A number of roles have been put forth for librarians in relation to MOOCs; librarians can work with copyright issues, support the production of MOOCs and the students taking them, assess MOOCs, and preserve and create content for them.[15] Another interesting occurrence has been librarians participating in MOOCs as learners, which can help librarians create empathy with students. Also, librarians create and teach MOOCs on numerous library and library-related topics. Nora Almeida, wring for the blog *In the Library with the Lead Pipe*, sees the role with MOOCs this way:

> We can begin by engaging with other institutional and community stakeholders and by building flexible infrastructures for information delivery, rights management, instruction, and curricular support that can withstand and even improve in the face of change. Librarianship, which has undergone its fair share of "disruption" in the past

few decades, is a field that is (perhaps uniquely) primed for change. In the context of online instruction, librarians have new opportunities to expand the realm of their work. In practice, this may mean taking on more active roles as co-instructors and content creators, educating faculty about open access scholarship, authoring best practice guidelines for intellectual property management, facilitating intra and inter institutional networks, or developing new controlled vocabularies and preservation protocols for archiving and repurposing MOOCs.[16]

Joseph Janes edited the book *Library 2020: Today's Leading Visionaries Describe Tomorrow's Library*, which offers numerous prognostications about where libraries and librarians are headed. In the section devoted to the subject heading "people," Stephen Abrams states, "A key service of librarians in 2020 is the personal-information consultation—more far-reaching than a traditional transactional reference but based in the transformational underpinned by good research and content"[17] and "librarians . . . continue to deliver value. Of course, that value is based even more on personal relationships and designing experiences for information users."[18] Courtney Greene concludes her chapter by stating, "Without question, librarianship is more than just the tools we use or the technology we teach. It may look, sound, or dress a bit differently from era to era, but I posit that both its future and its foundation rely on prioritizing the personal connection."[19] Lynn Silipigni Connaway sums up her contribution to the "community" section of the book, stating, "The library of 2020 will provide user-centered services and systems that will meet the expectations of the community. The library staff will need to develop relationships with their users and partner with other organizations in order to produce, store, and preserve content and data sets and to provide personalized services."[20] If this book and these views are any indication of what may transpire in libraries in the next six years, then personal librarian programs will surely be essential.

BUILDING A PERSONAL LIBRARIAN MIND-SET AND PROGRAM

In an informal perusal, roughly forty academic libraries appeared to market a personal librarian program (or an approximation) on their library websites. A number of these programs are mentioned throughout this book, including some that no longer exist. A question raised in chapter 3 about the relatively sparse adoption of personal librarian programs can lead to discussion and insight. Two reasons for not instituting this type of program might be a fear of duplicating services that are already in place under a different name and the idea that a personal librarian initiative is merely a promotional ploy. Yet authors in this book have put forth evidence that a personal librarian program can be implemented with elements that are currently in place and perhaps adding or mixing in some of the other ideas mentioned from other programs. The important takeaway is that the program should be marketed to students as a directed and dedicated effort to help them and, furthermore (although it does not need to be spelled out), form supportive relationships with librarians.

Several designs emerge when exploring the different ways in which libraries construct their mapping of students to librarians. Some of these pairings have been touched on in earlier chapters, and it is interesting to consider the methods that are used. The most common is dividing up students alphabetically and pairing them with a librarian, yet there are other inventive systems. For example, the University of Iowa uses Living–Learning Communities in their First-Year Experience program to match students with personal librarians. In a similar way, Barnard Library uses a Constellation grouping that is tied to the dorms. Duke University Libraries has a Residence Hall Librarian Program. Whether their focus is on first-generation students, transfer students, international students, or adult students, different institutions have found ways to reach out to various groups and make concentrated efforts to personalize those contacts. And why stop there? Why not personal librarians for faculty, staff, alumni, parents? Although his comments are addressed to the changes that occurred at the reference desk, David Tyckoson's observations can apply to personal librarian initiatives as well:

> Today's communities are much more diverse ethnically, racially, linguistically, and economically than those of a century ago. As a community changes, the library must redesign itself to meet the needs of the new demographics. The librarian needs to establish personal relations with each new generation of community members, even when that generation speaks Spanish, Mandarin, or Punjabi. The librarian also needs to serve the community wherever it is located, whether in the library, at home, at work, or traveling around the globe.[21]

The majority of this book on personal librarian programs centered on specific cases in the United States. However, a number of approaches are used elsewhere. In the book *Personalising Library Services in Higher Education: The Boutique Approach*, Andy Priestner and Elizabeth Tilley offer a similar alternative to personal librarian programs modeled on the idea of boutique hotels, which "can generally be characterized by the offering of a seamlessly intuitive and highly personalised service focusing on every detail of a guest's stay."[22] The authors, who are from the University of Cambridge, put together ways in which to implement their ideas as part of various aspects of librarianship along with case studies of how libraries around the world are personalizing services. Their discussion hints at the potential to apply the boutique model found in the hotel industry to the personalization of library services. Tilley defines boutique libraries as those having these eight qualities:

1. Subject specialism
2. Customer focused
3. Highly tailored
4. Trend-setting and reactive
5. High degree of autonomy
6. Unique services and resources
7. Personalized
8. Convenient location[23]

It is easy to see how customer-focused, personalized, trend-setting, unique, and highly tailored traits map to personal librarian goals. The University of Toronto has a very robust three-year personal librarian program and intends to reach out to all 7,000 of their incoming students in the future. They are also leaders when assessing the use and value of their personal librarian program, offering valuable insight for other institutions.

One other trepidation that is often expressed in discussions of implementing a personal librarian program is the effect it will have on staff time. Although this has been addressed to some extent in this book, another factor to consider is that, by most metrics, it can be difficult to assess the impact of a personal librarian program, but, commonly, the overall uptick in added work appears to be minimal.

Finally, a number of intangible yet positive results can occur by implementing a personal librarian program. Besides the ones put forth in earlier chapters, such as lowering library anxiety and students gaining better knowledge of librarians and their services, there is also the increased opportunities for self-directed and informal learning. When students see or feel as though librarians have made an effort to reach out to them and have shown great effort to point out how they are also invested in students' education, then a different mind-set might develop. Librarians' empathetic gestures can also go a long way toward students developing trust in and reliance on them. Many of the more daunting academic librarian–led encounters, such as information literacy lectures and lists of abundant physical and virtual resources, can be reinvigorated when students feel a warm rush of security upon seeing the words *personal librarian*, disconcerting as this may be to some librarians. Sometimes easy-to-grasp, simple ideas have more impact than the best planned standards.

CONCLUSION

All of the preceding issues and concerns were addressed at the First National Personal Librarian and First Year Experience Library Conference at Case Western Reserve University in Cleveland, Ohio, in April 2014. This two-day event showcased plenary, poster, and breakout sessions from librarians at small, medium, and large institutions and dealt with matters such as how first-year programming can be tied to personal librarian programs and how personal librarian programs bring staff librarians together and build camaraderie. This conference is hopefully a harbinger of things to come, showing how the interest in, and increasing popularity of, personal librarian programs is a growing topic for librarians.

Moving from placing the importance on resources to prioritizing relationships is not always an easy shift for a librarian. Certainly, a librarian can also be considered a "resource." Yet the conception of librarians as static information sentinels must be replaced with the image of librarians as active links between people and dynamic creation. Writing in the blog *Not So Distant Future*, about technology, libraries, and schools, Carolyn Foote puts forth this idea: "So perhaps it is time we turn the notion of 'collection development' into 'connection' development. And wasn't that always really the point anyway?—not the collection itself, but the connections it allowed our customers (students, teachers) to make; although the focus has too often been more on the collection than on the people involved."[24]

In his presentation titled "Collaborate! (Is There Any Other Way?)," David Shumaker quotes Jessamyn West by way of David Lankes: "When people have an information need, they'll always ask people they know before they ask a librarian. The trick is making sure that some of the people they know are librarians."[25] This trick can occur when the personal librarian enhances the student experience.

NOTES

1. Bell, "From Gatekeepers to Gate-Openers," 51.
2. Ibid.
3. Ibid., 53.
4. Middleton and Tucker, "Developing Community-Led Training," 11.
5. Pateman and Williment, *Developing Community-Led Public Libraries*, 2.
6. "RLUK Redefining the Research Library Model."
7. "WAPL Recap."
8. Fister, "Decode Academy," 2.
9. "Augustana Human Library."
10. "What Is the Human Library?"
11. Ibid.

12. Pink, *Whole New Mind*.
13. Barnett, *Libraries, Community, and Technology*, 27.
14. Neal, "Advancing from Kumbaya to Radical Collaboration."
15. Schwartz, "Massive Open Opportunity."
16. Almeida, "New Polemic."
17. Janes, *Library 2020*, 45.
18. Ibid.
19. Ibid., 53.
20. Ibid., 86.
21. Tyckoson, "On the Desirableness of Personal Relations," 15.
22. Priestner and Tilley, *Personalising Library Services*, 3.
23. Tilley, "Boutique Libraries at Your Service."
24. Foote, "Paradigm Shift?"
25. Shumaker, "Collaborate!"

BIBLIOGRAPHY

Almeida, Nora. "A New Polemic: Libraries, MOOCs, and the Pedagogical Landscape." *In the Library with the Lead Pipe* (blog), August 21, 2013. www.inthelibrarywiththeleadpipe.org/2013/a-new-polemic-libraries-moocs-and-the-pedagogical-landscape.

"Augustana Human Library." University of Alberta Libraries. Accessed August 13, 2013. www.library.ualberta.ca/augustana/infolit/humanlibrary.

Barnett, Andy. *Libraries, Community, and Technology*. Jefferson, NC: McFarland, 2002.

Bell, Steven. "From Gatekeepers to Gate-Openers." *American Libraries* 40, no. 8/9 (2009): 50–53.

Fister, Barbara. "Decode Academy." Talk presented at the Annual LOEX Conference, Nashville, TN, May 3, 2013. http://homepages.gac.edu/~fister/loex13.pdf.

Foote, Carolyn. "A Paradigm Shift—'Connection' Development?" *Not So Distant Future* (blog), January 6, 2011. http://futura.edublogs.org/2011/01/06/a-paradigm-shift-connection-development.

Green, Samuel S. "Personal Relations between Librarians and Readers." *Library Journal* 1 (1876): 74–81.

Janes, Joseph. *Library 2020: Today's Leading Visionaries Describe Tomorrow's Library*. New York: Scarecrow Press, 2013.

Middleton, S., and S. Tucker. "Developing Community-Led Training: Putting Principles into Practice." *Feliciter* 59, no. 2 (2013): 10–11.

Neal, Jim G. "Advancing from Kumbaya to Radical Collaboration: Redefining the Future Research Library." *Journal of Library Administration* 51, no. 1 (2011): 66–76. doi:10.1080/01930826.2011.531642.

Pateman, John, and Ken Williment. *Developing Community-Led Public Libraries: Evidence from the UK and Canada.* Farnham, Surrey, UK: Ashgate, 2013.

Pink, Daniel. *A Whole New Mind: Why Right-Brainers Will Rule the Future.* New York: Riverhead Books, 2006.

Priestner, Andy, and Elizabeth Tilley. *Personalising Library Services in Higher Education: The Boutique Approach.* Farnham, Surrey, UK: Ashgate, 2012.

"RLUK Redefining the Research Library Model." Research Libraries UK. Accessed August 13, 2013. http://rlukrrlm.wordpress.com/2012/09/01/services-and -staff.

Schwartz, Meredith. "Massive Open Opportunity: Supporting MOOCs in Public and Academic Libraries." *Library Journal,* May 10, 2013. http://lj.libraryjournal .com/2013/05/library-services/massive-open-opportunity-supporting-moocs.

Shumaker, David. "Collaborate! (Is There Any Other Way?)." Slideshow presentation at the Special Libraries Association Annual Conference, San Diego, CA, June 11, 2013. www.slideshare.net/davidshumaker/sla-panel-oncollaboration11june 2013shumaker.

Tilley, Elizabeth. "Boutique Libraries at Your Service." Academia.edu. July 2010. www.academia.edu/625703/Boutique_libraries_at_your_service.

Tyckoson, David. "On the Desirableness of Personal Relations between Librarians and Readers: The Past and Future of Reference Service." *Reference Services Review* 31, no. 1 (2003): 12–16.

"A WAPL Recap." Library as Incubator Project. May 13, 2012. www.libraryasincubator project.org/?p=4594.

"What Is the Human Library?" Human Library. Accessed August 12, 2013. http:// humanlibrary.org/what-is-the-living-library.html.

About the Editors and Contributors

RICHARD MONIZ holds a Doctorate in Higher Education Administration from Florida International University, a Master of Library and Information Science from the University of Rhode Island, and a Master of Arts (History) from Rhode Island College. He has served as a Director of Library Services for Johnson & Wales for the past seventeen years (seven years in North Miami, Florida, and ten in Charlotte, North Carolina). He has also served as an adjunct instructor for the University of North Carolina at Greensboro's Graduate School of Education for the past seven years. His publications include articles in the following: *Library Leadership and Management*, *College and Undergraduate Libraries*, *Community and Junior College Libraries*, *North Carolina Libraries*, and *Library Journal*. He is sole author of the book *Practical and Effective Management of Libraries: Integrating Case Studies, General Management Theory, and Self-Understanding*. He is also a coauthor of the recently published *Fundamentals for the Academic Liaison* (alongside Jo Henry and Joe Eshleman). In addition, he has a contributed chapter in *Mid-Career Library and Information Professionals: A Leadership Primer*. Conference presentations include the Lilly Conference on College and University Teaching (2011 and 2012), American

Library Association Annual Meeting (2009, 2010, and 2012), and several for Metrolina Library Association dating back to 2006. Richard lives in Charlotte with his wife, Lisa (also a librarian), and their children, Chris, Jamey, Riley, and Kevin.

JEAN MOATS, Librarian, has a Master of Library Science from the University of North Carolina at Greensboro, a Bachelor of Arts in Home Economics and Business from Otterbein College, and a Master of Divinity in Pastoral Ministry from Duke Divinity School. Prior to the library degree, Jean worked as a pastry chef for several local catering companies while earning a degree in Culinary Arts and Hotel/Restaurant Management from Central Piedmont Community College in Charlotte, North Carolina. She worked in the Technical Services Department at Queens University of Charlotte while earning her MLS from UNC at Greensboro. Jean joined the library staff of Johnson & Wales University in Charlotte in August 2004 and is a liaison for the College of Culinary Arts. Other responsibilities include cataloging materials, staffing the reference desk, and teaching information literacy sessions. Jean is a member of the American Library Association, Metrolina Library Association, North Carolina Library Association, Society of North Carolina Archivists, Society of American Archivists, Association for the Study of Food and Society, and the Food, Agriculture, and Nutrition Division of the Special Libraries Association.

■ ■ ■

Joe Eshleman received his Master of Library and Information Science from the University of North Carolina at Greensboro in 2007. He has been the Instruction Librarian at Johnson & Wales University Library–Charlotte since 2008. During this time, he has taught numerous library instruction sessions. Mr. Eshleman completed the Association of College and Research Libraries' Immersion Program, an intensive program of training and education for instruction librarians, in 2009. He is a coauthor of the recently published *Fundamentals for the Academic Liaison* (alongside Richard Moniz and Jo Henry). He has presented on numerous occasions, including the American Library Association Conference, the Lilly Education Conference, the Teaching Professor Technology Conference, and the First National Personal Librarian and First Year Experience Library Conference. Joe lives in Davidson, North Carolina, with his wife, Kristen, and their daughter, Grace.

Valerie Freeman, Librarian, has a Master of Library and Information Science from the University of North Carolina at Greensboro and a Bachelor of Arts in History from Kenyon College in Gambier, Ohio. She joined the staff at Johnson

& Wales University in August 2008 and is the liaison for the College of Business. She also participates in teaching information literacy classes, assists in cataloging, manages student workers, and coordinates service desks. She is a member of the American Library Association and North Carolina Library Association, in addition to the Metrolina Library Association, where she has served on the Board of Directors for five years.

Jo Henry is currently Information Services Librarian at South Piedmont Community College in Polkton, North Carolina. Formerly, she worked at Charlotte Mecklenburg Library in Charlotte, North Carolina, and she has over twenty years' experience in sports club management and instruction. She obtained a Master of Library and Information Science from the University of North Carolina at Greensboro and a Master of Public Administration from Georgia Southern University. She is the coauthor of *Fundamentals for the Academic Liaison* (alongside Richard Moniz and Joe Eshleman). She has also published in *Public Services Quarterly* and *Library Review*, and she has presented at the Metrolina Information Literacy Conference (2011, 2013, and 2014) and the North Carolina Library Association Bi-Annual Conference (2013). In addition, she serves as Treasurer for the Metrolina Library Association.

David Jewell holds a Doctorate in Health Science from Nova Southeastern University, a Master of Science in Nutrition from University of North Carolina at Chapel Hill, and a Master of Arts in Exercise Physiology from UNC–Chapel Hill. In addition, he has an American College of Sports Medicine (ACSM) certification. He has served as the College Chair of Arts and Sciences for Johnson & Wales University for the past four years, Math and Science Coordinator for three years prior to being College Chair, and nine years as a science faculty member. David has a beautiful and supportive family including his wife, Martie, and their four children, Victoria, Augustus, Maxten, and Annabelle.

Index

CPSIA information can be obtained at www.ICGtesting.com
Printed in the USA
LVOW07s1536020315

428936LV00020B/1584/P